Practice Book
Grade 1

Together Again

Join In

Special Times

Harcourt

Orlando   Boston   Dallas   Chicago   San Diego

Visit *The Learning Site!*

www.harcourtschool.com

Contents

TOGETHER AGAIN - THEME 1

TOGETHER AGAIN - THEME 2

Harcourt

Contents

JOIN IN

Harcourt

Contents

SPECIAL TIMES

Harcourt

Contents

Harcourt

Together
Again

Name _____

▶ **Finish each sentence. Write I and a.**

1. __I__ 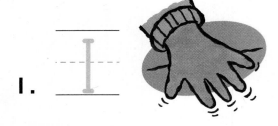 __a__  .

2. _____ 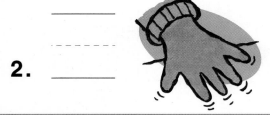 _____  .

3. _____  _____  .

4. _____ 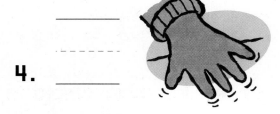 _____  .

Together Again Theme 1
Lesson 1

SCHOOL-HOME CONNECTION Ask your child to tell you
about the sentences he or she completed on this page.
Have your child point to the word *I* and then to the word *a*.

Harcourt

▶ **Say the name of the picture. Write m if the word begins with the /m/ sound.**

1.

_____
- - - - - - - - - - - - - -
_____

2.

_____
- - - - - - - - - - - - - -
_____

3.

_____
- - - - - - - - - - - - - -
_____

4.

_____
- - - - - - - - - - - - - -
_____

5.

_____
- - - - - - - - - - - - - -
_____

6.

_____
- - - - - - - - - - - - - -
_____

TRY THIS Use a crayon to print a big m. Use other colors to trace around the m. Say "M-M-M-M" as you work.

SCHOOL-HOME CONNECTION Ask your child to name the pictures that begin with the same sound as *milk*. Think of more words that begin with the same sound.

Together Again Theme 1
Lesson 1

9

Harcourt

Name _____

▶ **Say the name of each picture. Circle the picture if the name has the /a/ sound.**

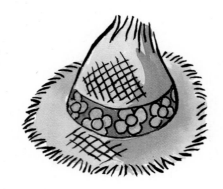

SCHOOL-HOME CONNECTION Ask your child to name the pictures whose names have short vowel *a*. Find at least one more object in the house whose name has the short *a* sound.

Harcourt

Name _____

▶ **Say a sentence to tell what happens in each picture.**

1.

2.

3.

4.

Harcourt

SCHOOL-HOME CONNECTION With your child say a few short sentences. Discuss that a sentence tells a complete thought.

Name _____

▶ **Write the word that best completes each sentence.**

<u>what house</u>

1. Here is the _____ .

_____

<u>the big</u>

2. Here is _____ .

_____

<u>Here The</u>

3. _____ is the _____ .

 TRY THIS What cat names can you think of that begin with <u>M</u>?

Harcourt

Name _____

house   **is**

_____

- - - - - - - - - - - - - - - -

4. Here _____ the  .

Here   **What**

_____

- - - - - - - - - - - - - - - -

5. _____ is here?

---

big   **am**

_____

- - - - - - - - - - - - - - - -

6. A _____  is here!

SCHOOL-HOME CONNECTION Ask your child to read
the sentences on these pages. Discuss with your child the
kinds of animals that people have as pets.

Together Again Theme 1
Lesson 2   **13**

Harcourt

Name _____

▶ **Name each picture. Circle the pictures whose names begin with /m/. Then write the letter m̲.**

1.

2.

3.

4.

▶ **Name each picture. Circle the pictures whose names have the /a/ sound. Then write the letter a̲.**

5.

6.

7.

8.

SCHOOL-HOME CONNECTION Have your child print *m* and *a* on scrap paper. Say *milk, hand, ant, moon, cap,* and *men.* Stop after each word and have your child point to the letter that stands for the sound they hear in the word.

Harcourt

Name _____

▶ **Think about the story. Draw a picture in each box to complete the story rhyme.**

SCHOOL-HOME CONNECTION Ask your child to use the pictures to tell you about the story *The Big Surprise*.

Together Again Theme 1
Lesson 2

Name _____

▶ **Say the name of the picture. Write s̲ on the line if the name begins with the /s/ sound.**

1.

_____

S

2.

_____

3.

_____

4.

_____

5.

_____

6.

_____

Together Again Theme 1
Lesson 3

SCHOOL-HOME CONNECTION *Make up an "s song"*
by singing words that begin with the s sound to a
tune your child knows.

Harcourt

Name _____

Phonics

Short Vowel: /a/a;
Consonants: /s/s,
/m/m

▶ **Say the name of the picture. Write m or s to show the beginning sound. Draw a circle around the pictures that show animals.**

1.  _____

2.  _____

3. 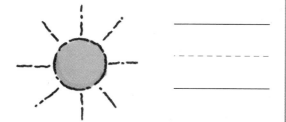 _____

4.  _____

▶ **Say the name of the picture. Write a if the name has the sound /a/. Draw a circle around the pictures that show animals.**

5. 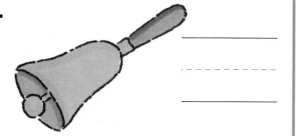 _____

6.  _____

7.  _____

8.  _____

Harcourt

SCHOOL-HOME CONNECTION Have your child print *s, a,* and *m* on scrap paper. Say *sit, men, cat,* and *Sam.* Stop after each word and have your child point to the letter that stands for the sound at the beginning of each word.

Name _____

▶ **The pictures are out of order. Write the number 1, 2, or 3 by each one to show which happened first, next, and last.**

_____ _____ _____

▶ **Draw what might happen next.**

Together Again Theme 1
Lesson 4

Harcourt

Name _____

▶ **Name each picture. If the name rhymes with <u>Sam</u>, write <u>am</u>.**

1.

_____

_ _ _ _ _ _ _ _ _

_____

2.

_____

_ _ _ _ _ _ _ _ _

_____

3.

_____

_ _ _ _ _ _ _ _ _

_____

4.

_____

_ _ _ _ _ _ _ _ _

_____

5.

_____

_ _ _ _ _ _ _ _ _

_____

6.

_____

_ _ _ _ _ _ _ _ _

_____

▶ **Draw a picture of yourself. Then finish the sentence.**

_____

_ _ _ _ _ _ _ _ _

I am _____.

SCHOOL-HOME CONNECTION Ask your child to name the pictures that end with the same sounds you can hear at the end of *Sam*. Together, make up a short poem with two of the words.

Together Again Theme 1
Lesson 5   **19**

Name _____

▶ **Say the name of the picture. Write t if the name begins or ends with the /t/ sound.**

1.

_____
- - - - - - - - - - - -
_____

2.

_____
- - - - - - - - - - - -
_____

3.

_____
- - - - - - - - - - - -
_____

4.

_____
- - - - - - - - - - - -
_____

5.

_____
- - - - - - - - - - - -
_____

6.

_____
- - - - - - - - - - - -
_____

TRY THIS Draw a picture of a teddy bear. Draw a cap on the teddy bear and write T on it. Give your teddy bear a name that begins with T.

Together Again Theme 1
Lesson 6

SCHOOL-HOME CONNECTION Find ten things in your house whose names begin with the sound t stands for.

Harcourt

Name _____

▶ **Circle each word group that is a sentence. Then write the sentence.**

is where   Here I am.   Sam Sam

Where is Sam?   is where   Sam is here.

_____

1. _____

_____

2. _____

_____

3. _____

 TRY THIS Write a sentence about yourself.
Draw a picture, too.

SCHOOL-HOME CONNECTION Let your child point
out sentences on this page or in a book. Ask where
one sentence ends and the next sentence begins.

Together Again Theme 1
Lesson 6

Harcourt

Name _____

▶ **Write the word from the box that best completes each sentence.**

| Come | Where | in | are |

1. _____ is Sam?

2. Is Sam _____ the house?

3. _____ here, Sam.

4. Where _____ you?

SCHOOL-HOME CONNECTION Talk about what the word *in* means. Ask your child to name three things that are *in* his or her room.

Harcourt

▶ **Write the word from the box that best completes each sentence.**

that	come	look	You

_____

1. I _____ at Sam.

_____

2. I look at _____ big, big cat.

_____

3. _____ are a fat cat.

_____

4. You can _____ in here.

TRY THIS Where would you look if you couldn't find your cat? Draw three places you might look.

Harcourt

Phonics

Short Vowel: /a/a
Consonants: /t/t,
/m/m

▶ **Say the name of the picture. Write t or m to show the beginning sound.**

1. _____

2. _____

3. _____

4. _____

▶ **Say the name of the picture. Write a if the name has the /a/ sound.**

5. _____

6. _____

7. _____

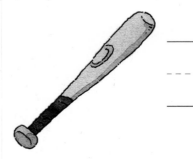

8. _____

Together Again Theme 1
Lesson 7

SCHOOL-HOME CONNECTION Have your child print *t*, *a*, and *m* on separate pieces of scrap paper. Say *at*, *am*, and *mat*. Have your child use the letters to spell each word.

Harcourt

▶ Think about the story. Read each sentence. Draw a picture to show where the girl looks for Tiger.

1. "Is Tiger here?"

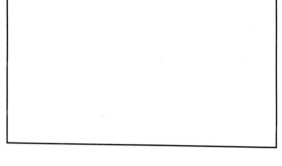

2. "Is Tiger here?"

3. "Is Tiger here?"

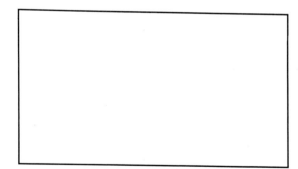

4. "Is Tiger here?"

SCHOOL-HOME CONNECTION Let your child tell you where the girl finds Tiger in the story *Come Here, Tiger*. Ask him or her to use this page to retell the story.

Together Again Theme 1
Lesson 7   **25**

Name _____

▶ **Name each picture. Write <u>c</u> if the name of the picture begins with the /k/ sound.**

1.
_____
_ _ _ _ _ _
C
_____

2.
_____
_ _ _ _ _ _
_____

3.
_____
_ _ _ _ _ _
_____

4.
_____
_ _ _ _ _ _
_____

5.
_____
_ _ _ _ _ _
_____

6.
_____
_ _ _ _ _ _
_____

7.
_____
_ _ _ _ _ _
_____

8.
_____
_ _ _ _ _ _
_____

TRY THIS Write your own sentence about something you need. Draw a picture to go with your sentence.

Together Again Theme 1
Lesson 8

SCHOOL-HOME CONNECTION Look out the window. Count the number of cars you see.

Harcourt

Name _____

▶ **Name each picture. Circle the pictures whose names begin with the /k/ sound. Then write the letter <u>c</u>.**

1.

c

_____

2.

_____

3.

_____

4.

_____

5.

_____

6.

_____

▶ **Read the words in the box. Write each word under the correct picture.**

mat   cat

7.

_____

8.

_____

SCHOOL-HOME CONNECTION Write the word *cat*, and let your child read the word to you. Together, think of other words that begin with the same sound you hear at the beginning of *cat*.

Together Again Theme 1
Lesson 9

27

Harcourt

Name _____

▶ **Write 1, 2, or 3 to put the pictures in order. Then write the sentences in order.**

_____   _____   _____

Here, Cat.   Look at Cat!   Come, Cat.

1. _____

2. _____

3. _____

Together Again Theme 1
Lesson 9

Harcourt

Name _____

▶ **Name each picture. If the name rhymes with <u>Sam</u>, write <u>am</u>. If the name rhymes with <u>cat</u>, write <u>at</u>.**

1.

_____

- - - - - - - - - - - - -

_____

2.

_____

- - - - - - - - - - - - -

_____

3.

_____

- - - - - - - - - - - - -

_____

4.

_____

- - - - - - - - - - - - -

_____

5.

_____

- - - - - - - - - - - - -

_____

6.

_____

- - - - - - - - - - - - -

_____

SCHOOL-HOME CONNECTION Say the tongue twister *Hide the ham in Heidi's hat.* Ask your child which word ends with *–am* and which word ends with *–at*. Then say the tongue twister together, as fast as you can.

Together Again Theme 1
Lesson 10

Harcourt

▶ **Name each picture. Write the letter p if the name begins with the /p/ sound.**

1.

p

2.

3.

4.

5.

6.

7.

8.

9.

TRY THIS Draw a picture of something whose name begins with p. Color it purple or pink even if it looks silly.

30

Together Again Theme 1
Lesson 11

SCHOOL-HOME CONNECTION Hunt through
the house for things that are purple or pink.

Harcourt

Name _____

▶ **Silly Sam's words are all mixed up. Write the words in order.**

1. I Sam. am

_____

- - - - - - - - - - - - - - - - - - - -

_____

2. sat I here.

_____

- - - - - - - - - - - - - - - - - - - -

_____

3. here. sat Matt

_____

- - - - - - - - - - - - - - - - - - - -

_____

4. cat here. A sat

_____

- - - - - - - - - - - - - - - - - - - -

_____

TRY THIS Draw a picture of yourself. Make up a sentence about it. Say your words in order.

 SCHOOL-HOME CONNECTION Say a short sentence. Mix up the order of two words in your sentence. Ask your child to say the sentence with the words in the right order.

Together Again Theme 1
Lesson 11   **31**

Harcourt

Name _____

▶ **Write a word to complete each sentence. Write one letter in each box.**

run   good   to   me

1. Run ☐☐ Mat.

2. Now ☐☐☐ to Pat.

3. Come to ☐☐ !

4. You are ☐☐☐☐ !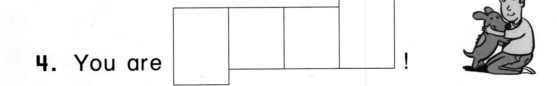

TRY THIS Think of a word that rhymes with <u>Mat</u> and <u>Pat</u>. Write your word, but mix up the letters. Give your paper to a friend. He or she can try to write the word correctly.

Harcourt

Name _____

► **Write a word to complete each sentence. Write one letter in each box.**

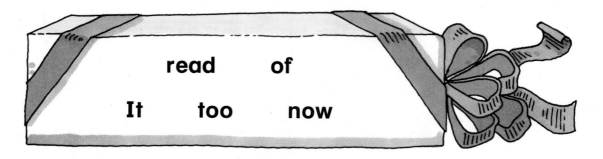

read   of

It   too   now

1. Come here ⬚⬚⬚ .

2. Look at me ⬚⬚⬚⬚ .

3. It is a 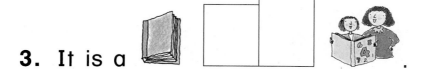 ⬚⬚ .

4. ⬚⬚ is a big  .

5. Come read it, ⬚⬚⬚ .

Harcourt

Name _____

Phonics

Short Vowel: /a/a
Consonants: /p/p,
/t/t

▶ **Say the name of each picture. Color the oval pink if the name begins with /p/. Color the oval green if the name begins with /t/. Color the oval blue if the name has the /a/ sound.**

SCHOOL-HOME CONNECTION With your child, write a silly story about a pig named Pat. Have your child circle words that contain the letter *p*.

Harcourt

Name _____

▶ **Think about the story. Look at the pictures. Circle <u>YES</u> if the picture shows something the children in the story do. Circle <u>NO</u> if it shows something that did not happen.**

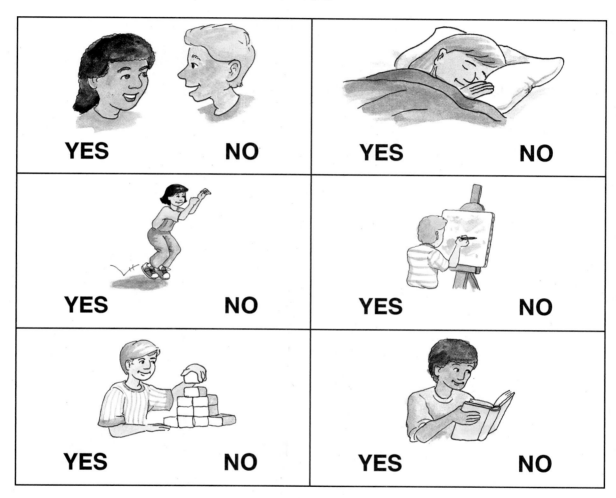

YES   NO   YES   NO

YES   NO   YES   NO

YES   NO   YES   NO

Now write what you liked best in the story.

_____

_ _

_____

_ _

_____

SCHOOL-HOME CONNECTION Have your child tell you about the activities the children in *Look At Me* were doing. Encourage your child to describe some things he or she can do.

Together Again Theme 1
Lesson 12   **35**

Harcourt

Name _____

▶ **Name each picture. Write the letter h if the name begins with the sound /h/.**

1.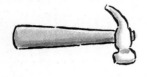

h

2.

3.

4.

5.

6.

7.

8.

9.

TRY THIS Put your hand on a sheet of paper. Open your fingers and trace your hand. Draw a picture of something you are happy about.

SCHOOL-HOME CONNECTION Ask your child to draw a picture of your home. Help him or her write your address on the picture.

Harcourt

Name _____

▶ **Look at each picture. Write the word that best completes each sentence.**

ham	mat	sat	has	hat

1. Here is the _____.

2. Is that the _____?

3. Where is the _____?

4. Pam _____ the map.

5. Pat _____.

Harcourt

SCHOOL-HOME CONNECTION Write a list of things you would pack for a trip to the beach. Have your child point out any words that contain the short *a*, *s*, or *h* sounds.

Name _____

▶ **Finish each sentence. Add s to the word above the line. Write that new word on the line.**

come

_____

- - - - - - - - - - -

1. Here _____ Sam.

pat

_____

- - - - - - - - - - -

2. Pam _____ Sam.

cat

_____

- - - - - - - - - - -

3. Here come the _____.

look

_____

- - - - - - - - - - -

4. Sam _____ at the cats.

meow

_____

- - - - - - - - - - -

5. The red cat _____ at Sam.

SCHOOL-HOME CONNECTION Write the words *hat* and *hats*. Ask your child to tell you how the two words are different. With your child, make up a sentence using both words.

Harcourt

Name _____

▶ **Name each picture. If the name rhymes with <u>tap</u>, write <u>ap</u>. If the name rhymes with <u>sat</u>, write <u>at</u>.**

1.

_____

— — — — — — —

_____

2.

_____

— — — — — — —

_____

3.

_____

— — — — — — —

_____

4.

_____

— — — — — — —

_____

5.

_____

— — — — — — —

_____

6.

_____

— — — — — — —

_____

7.

_____

— — — — — — —

_____

8.

_____

— — — — — — —

_____

9.

_____

— — — — — — —

_____

Harcourt

▶ **Write the word from the box that best completes each sentence.**

dad	sad	mad	had	pad

_____

1. I am _____ .

_____

2. I am _____ .

_____

3. I _____ a cap.

_____

4. I see the _____ .

_____

5. I see my _____ .

SCHOOL-HOME CONNECTION Ask your child to read aloud the words in the box. Have him or her tell you which letter is at the end of each word. Encourage your child to name familiar objects that begin with the *d* sound.

Harcourt

Name _____

▶ **Write these telling sentences correctly.**

1. look at that

_____

- -

_____

2. that cat has a big hat

_____

- -

_____

3. i see a cat

_____

- -

_____

4. the cat has a cap

_____

- -

_____

- -

_____

 TRY THIS Write a telling sentence about your favorite pet.

 SCHOOL-HOME CONNECTION Ask your child to say a few sentences about a cat. Write the sentences. Have your child point out the capital letters and periods.

Together Again Theme 2
Lesson 1

41

Name _____

▶ **Write the words from the box where they belong on the rainbow.**

red	green	yellow

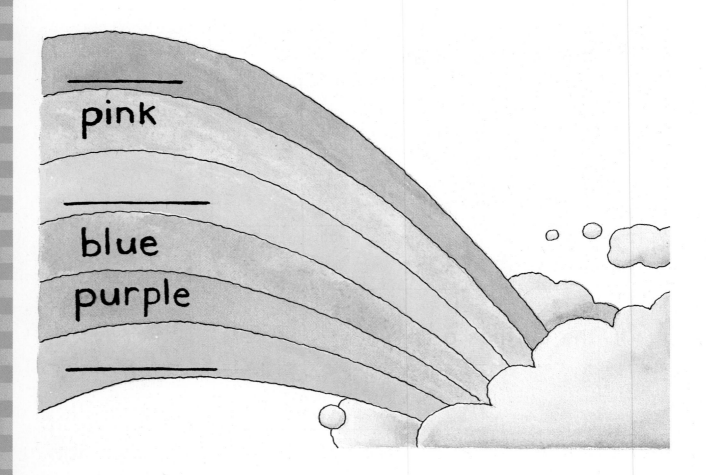

pink

blue
purple

Harcourt

 TRY THIS What is your favorite color? Write it. Then draw something and color it your favorite color.

Name _____

▶ **Write the word from the box that best completes each sentence.**

black	brown	see	red

1. I _____ a green hat.

_____

2. I see a _____ hat.

_____

3. That hat is _____.

_____

4. Here is a big _____

hat.

Harcourt

Name _____

▶ **Write the word from the box that best completes the sentence.**

see	walking	went	saw

_____

- - - - - - - - - - - - - - - - -

1. I am _____ .

_____

- - - - - - - - - - - - - - - - -

2. I _____ Pam and Pat.

_____

- - - - - - - - - - - - - - - - -

3. I _____ walking.

_____

- - - - - - - - - - - - - - - - -

4. I _____ Pam and Pat.

SCHOOL-HOME CONNECTION Write the words *see* and *saw*, and ask your child to read the words aloud. Then ask your child to name something he or she can *see* right now, and something he or she *saw* at school earlier.

Harcourt

Name _____

Phonics
Consonants: /d/d, /h/h
Short Vowel: /a/a

▶ **Write the word from the box that names each picture.**

| ham | hats | dad | pads | map | cats |

1. _____

2. _____

3. _____

4. _____

5. _____

6. _____

Harcourt

SCHOOL-HOME CONNECTION Ask your child to say some words that begin with the same sound as *horse*.

Name _____

▶ **Think about the story. Draw a line
through the maze to show things that happened.
Then retell the story to a friend.**

Together Again Theme 2
Lesson 2

Harcourt

▶ **Name each picture. Listen for the sound in the middle of the word. Write i if you hear the sound /i/.**

1. _____

2. _____

3. _____

4. _____

5. _____

6. _____

7. _____

8. _____

9. _____

SCHOOL-HOME CONNECTION Ask your child to identify the letter that stands for the beginning sound in the word *igloo*. Have your child practice writing that letter.

Together Again Theme 2
Lesson 3

Harcourt

Name _____

▶ **Write the words where they belong in the puzzle.**

| hit | tip | pat | pit | pad |

1.

2.

3.

4.

5.

1. ↓

3. ↓

2. →

5. ↓

4. →

Together Again Theme 2
Lesson 4

SCHOOL-HOME CONNECTION Ask what sound your child hears in the middle of the word *sit*. Together, think of other words that have the same sound.

Harcourt

Name _____

▶ **Read each word. If the word names a color, color the space. If the word names an animal, do not color the space.**

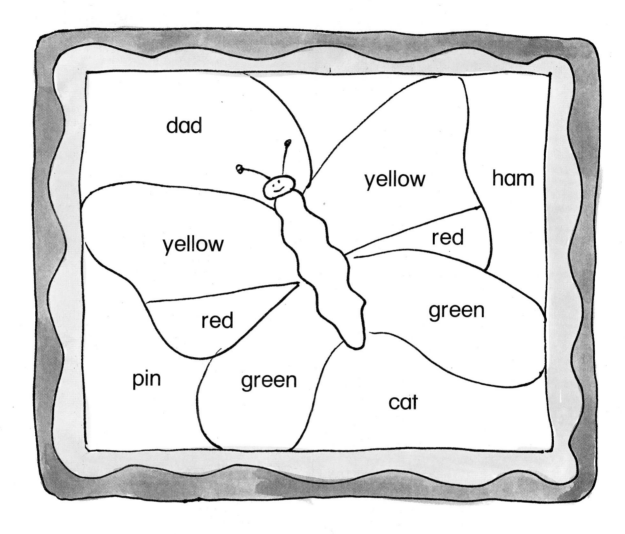

What is it?

TRY THIS What is your favorite color? Make a list of things that are that color.

SCHOOL-HOME CONNECTION Have your child sort household objects by size, shape, or color.

Together Again Theme 2
Lesson 4   49

Name _____

▶ **Look at each picture. Circle the word that completes the sentence. Then write the word.**

_____
- - - - - - - - - - - -

1. Here is _____.

Dad
Did
Mad

_____
- - - - - - - - - - - -

2. Dad _____ a mitt.

his
dad
had

_____
- - - - - - - - - - - -

3. I _____ his mitt.

mad
sit
hid

_____
- - - - - - - - - - - -

4. Dad is _____.

sat
sit
sad

_____
- - - - - - - - - - - -

5. I _____ it.

dad
did
mad

SCHOOL-HOME CONNECTION Ask your child to write the words *had* and *hid*. Let your child point out the letters that are the same and the letters that are different.

Harcourt

Name _____

▶ **Look at each picture. Circle the word that completes each sentence. Then write the word.**

1. Look _____ Tim.

it
at
pat

2. Tim is a _____.

mat
mitt
cat

3. Tim can _____.

sit
sat
pit

4. Tim has a _____.

hit
hat
it

5. _____ is red.

Hit
At
It

Harcourt

SCHOOL-HOME CONNECTION Ask your child to say three words that rhyme with *sit* and three words that rhyme with *sat*.

Together Again Theme 2
Lesson 5

51

► **Name each picture. Write n if the name begins or ends with the /n/ sound.**

1.	2.	3. 
n		
4. 	5. 	6. 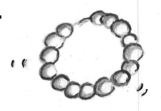
7. 	8. 	9. 

Together Again Theme 2
Lesson 6

SCHOOL-HOME CONNECTION With your child, think of other words that begin with the sound you hear at the beginning of *nap*. Then let your child practice writing the letter *n*.

Harcourt

Name _____

▶ **Write these asking sentences correctly.**

1. where is Sam

_____

- - - - - - - - - - - - - - - - - - - -

_____

2. can I come in?

_____

- - - - - - - - - - - - - - - - - - - -

_____

3. what did you see

_____

- - - - - - - - - - - - - - - - - - - -

_____

▶ **Read the sentences. Circle the asking sentence.**
Underline the telling sentence.

Where is the cat?   **The cat is in here.**

TRY THIS What do you want to know about dogs? Write your own asking sentence. Use a capital letter and a question mark.

 SCHOOL-HOME CONNECTION Help your child come up with asking sentences. Write the sentences, and have your child point out the capital letters and the question marks.

Together Again Theme 2
Lesson 6

53

Harcourt

Name _____

▶ **Write the word that best completes each sentence.**

Tim and Sam went walking.

up   of

_____

- - - - - - - - - - - - -

1. "Come _____ to see me," said  .

___

come   little

_____

- - - - - - - - - - - - -

2. "That house is too _____!" said Tim.

___

good   down

_____

- - - - - - - - - - - - -

3. "Come _____ to see me," said  .

___

saw   said

_____

- - - - - - - - - - - - -

4. "That house is too little," _____ Sam.

 **SCHOOL-HOME CONNECTION** Write the words *big* and *little* on a piece of paper. With your child, make lists of big animals and little animals.

Harcourt

Name _____

▶ **Write the word that best completes
each sentence.**

brown   back

_____

1. Tim went _____ to the big house.

going   good

_____

2. "Where are you _____?" said Sam.

make   mad

_____

3. "I am going to _____ a big ,"
    said Tim.

Get   Come

_____

4. "_____ a ," said Sam.

 **TRY
THIS** Draw a picture of something you like to make. Write
a sentence to go with the picture. Use the word
<u>make</u> in your sentence.

Name _____

Phonics
Short Vowel: /a/a
Consonants: /n/n, /d/d

▶ **Look at each picture. Circle the word that completes the sentence. Then write the word.**

1. I see a _____.   mad
   man
   nap

2. This man is my _____.   had
   did
   dad

3. My dad has a _____.   can
   cat
   hat

4. Here is the _____.   pad
   pan
   pin

5. My dad has a _____.   pin
   pad
   nap

Together Again Theme 2
Lesson 7

SCHOOL-HOME CONNECTION Have your child point to the word *man* on this page. Together, think of several words that rhyme with the word *man*.

Harcourt

Name _____

► **Think about the story. Draw pictures of
the two main characters. Write the characters'
names under your pictures. Then draw a picture
to show the ending.**

_____   _____

- - - - - - - - - - - - - - -   - - - - - - - - - - - - - - -

_____   _____

 SCHOOL-HOME CONNECTION Ask your child about the
story *Big Pig and Little Pig.* What surprises Big Pig? Have your
child tell what Little Pig does and how he must feel.

Together Again Theme 2
Lesson 22   **57**

Name _____

▶ **Name each picture. Write the word in the box that best names each picture.**

| kids | sack | kit | tack | kick | pack |

1.

_____

- - - - - - - - - - - -

_____

2.

_____

- - - - - - - - - - - -

_____

3.

_____

- - - - - - - - - - - -

_____

4.

_____

- - - - - - - - - - - -

_____

5.

_____

- - - - - - - - - - - -

_____

6.

_____

- - - - - - - - - - - -

_____

TRY THIS Write a word that begins or ends with the /k/ sound. Draw a picture to go with the word.

Together Again Theme 2
Lesson 8

SCHOOL-HOME CONNECTION Have your child point out words that begin and end with the /k/ sound. Together, think of other words that begin or end with that sound.

Harcourt

Name _____

Phonics

Short Vowel: /i/i
Consonants: /k/k,
ck, /n/n

▶ **Look at the pictures. Write the word in the box that best completes each sentence.**

| kick | Nick | pack | pick |

1.

_____

- - - - - - - - - - - - - -

Kip can _____ .

2.

_____

- - - - - - - - - - - - - -

_____ can nap.

3.

_____

- - - - - - - - - - - - - -

Pam can _____ .

4.

_____

- - - - - - - - - - - - - -

Dan can _____ .

SCHOOL-HOME CONNECTION Ask your child to point out the word *kick* on this page. Encourage your child to say other words that end with the same sound.

Together Again Theme 2
Lesson 9   **59**

Harcourt

▶ **Read the contractions in the box. Finish each sentence. Write the contraction for the two words that are above the line.**

| Here's | Pat's | It's | What's | That's |

Pat is

1. _____ here now.

Here is

2. _____ my sack.

What is

3. _____ in it?

That is

4. _____ a surprise.

It is

5. _____ a good surprise.

SCHOOL-HOME CONNECTION Let your child point to two words he or she wrote as a contraction. Help your child think of other pairs of words that can be written together the same way.

Harcourt

Name _____

▶ **Write the naming part of each sentence.**

1. Mick sits here.

_____

- - - - - - - - - - - - - - -

_____

2. Pam can sit on that.

_____

- - - - - - - - - - - - - - -

_____

3. My dad can sit here.

_____

- - - - - - - - - - - - - - -

_____

4. Matt can sit here.

_____

- - - - - - - - - - - - - - -

_____

5. His dog can not sit here.

_____

- - - - - - - - - - - - - - -

_____

TRY THIS Choose one of the naming parts you wrote. Use it to begin another sentence. Write the new sentence.

 SCHOOL–HOME CONNECTION Encourage your child to tell you what the naming part of a sentence does. Then have your child say several sentences with the naming part *I*.

Together Again Theme 2
Lesson 11 **63**

Harcourt

Name _____

▶ **Write the word that tells about the toy in each box.**

| one | all | three | two | not | on |

red cats

green cat

yellow cats

the cats

the mat

on the mat

Harcourt

Name _____

▶ **Write the word from the box that completes each sentence.**

want	have	came	help	again

1. I _____ to kick.

2. Can you _____ me?

3. I _____ to help you.

4. Do you _____ it?

5. I can kick _____!

SCHOOL-HOME CONNECTION Write the word *help*, and have your child read it aloud. Then ask your child to name at least three ways in which he or she can help other people.

Harcourt

▶ **Write the word from the box that completes the sentence.**

lid	lap	lick	pal	hill

1. Pip can _____.

2. The _____ looks good to Pip.

3. Pip comes down the _____.

4. Pip sits on my _____.

5. Pip is my _____.

SCHOOL-HOME CONNECTION Let your child read aloud the words in the box. Ask which words begin with the sound /l/. Then ask which words end with the same sound.

Harcourt

Name _____

▶ **Match the story parts. Then retell the
story using the pictures and sentences.**

In the beginning • • Humpty Dumpty
comes down off the
wall.

In the middle • • Animals come
to help him.

At the end • • Humpty Dumpty
sat on a wall.

SCHOOL-HOME CONNECTION Let your child tell you what
happens in the beginning, middle, and at the end of the story
The Big Big Wall. Have him or her explain why Humpty Dumpty
was happy at the end of the story.

Together Again Theme 2
Lesson 12

Harcourt

▶ **Circle the word that completes each sentence. Then write the word.**

_____

- - - - - - - - - - - - -

1. The dogs are in the _____ .

hill
hall
call

_____

- - - - - - - - - - - -

2. Can _____ the dogs pass?

call
all
ill

_____

- - - - - - - - - - -

3. One dog is too _____ .

lit
tall
all

_____

- - - - - - - - - -

4. I _____ that dog Mack.

call
ill
mall

_____

- - - - - - - - - -

5. Where are _____ the dogs now?

hall
mall
all

SCHOOL-HOME CONNECTION Ask your child to write the word *all*. Together, think of words that rhyme with *all*.

Harcourt

Name _____

▶ **Circle the word that completes each sentence. Then write the word.**

_____

- - - - - - - - - - - - - -

1. Look at that _____ .

can
hat
cat

_____

_____

- - - - - - - - - - - - - -

2. He is _____ .

all
tall
call

_____

- - - - - - - - - - - - - -

3. That cat has _____ the hats.

a
at
all

_____

- - - - - - - - - - - - - -

4. One cat is in the _____ .

hat
hall
call

_____

- - - - - - - - - - - - - -

5. I can _____ the cat.

call
cat
can

Harcourt

SCHOOL-HOME CONNECTION Ask your child to point out at least three words that end with the letters *-all*. Together, think of other words that end with that same sound.

▶ **Look at the first animal in each row.**
Circle the other animals that are like the first one.

1.

2.

3.

4.

5.

SCHOOL-HOME CONNECTION With your child, sort the animals
on the page by new attributes, such as color, number of legs, and
feathers or fur.

▶ **Finish each sentence. Write the contraction for the two words.**

didn't	isn't	don't	hasn't	aren't

is   not
_____

- - - - - - - - - - - - - - -

1. Tim _____ here.

did   not
_____

- - - - - - - - - - - - - - -

2. He _____ call me.

are   not
_____

- - - - - - - - - - - - - - -

3. His pals _____ here.

do   not
_____

- - - - - - - - - - - - - - -

4. I _____ see it.

has   not
_____

- - - - - - - - - - - - - - -

5. It _____ come.

SCHOOL-HOME CONNECTION Let your child write the contraction
didn't. Ask which two words are joined in that contraction.

Together Again Theme 2
Lesson 15   **71**

▶ **Finish each sentence. Put together the word and the word ending. Write the new word.**

look + ed

_____

- - - - - - - - - - - - - - - - - - - -

1. Dan _____ for me.

look + ing

_____

- - - - - - - - - - - - - - - - - - - -

2. Now I am _____ for him.

call + ed

_____

- - - - - - - - - - - - - - - - - - - -

3. He _____ me.

call + ing

_____

- - - - - - - - - - - - - - - - - - - -

4. Now I am _____ him.

do + ing

_____

- - - - - - - - - - - - - - - - - - - -

5. What is Dan _____?

SCHOOL-HOME CONNECTION Have your child read aloud one of the sentences he or she completed. Ask how the word above the line changed. Encourage your child to make up other sentences using that word.

Harcourt

Sam

1

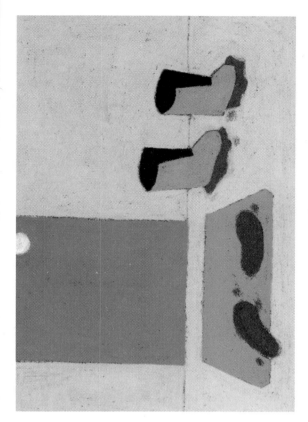

Is Sam here?

3

Fold

Harcourt

Fold

Here I am!

8

Is Sam here?

6

4

Is Sam here?

2

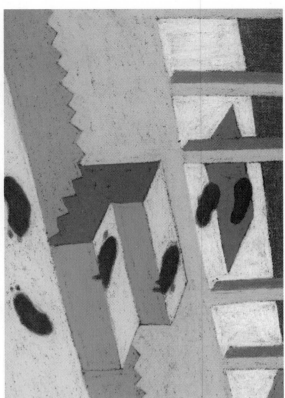

Is Sam here?

Fold

Fold

Harcourt

Is Sam here?

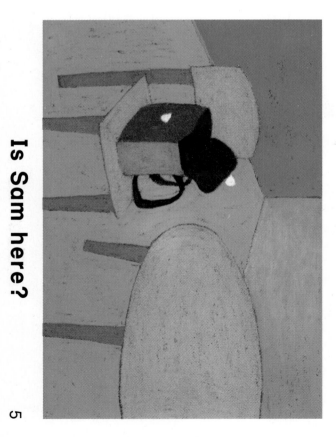

Is Sam here?

5

Is Sam here?

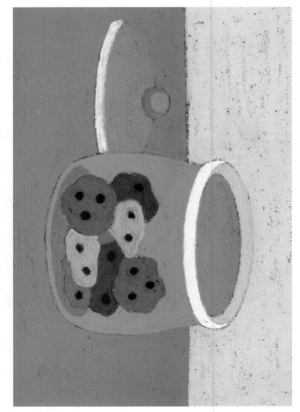

7

That Cat

1

8

Here is that cat.

Look at that cat!

3

Look, cat.

6

Fold

Fold

4

Where is that cat?

2

Look!

✂

Harcourt

Fold

Fold

Come, cat, come!

5

Come here, cat!

✂

7

Hap and Pam

Harcourt

Where is Hap?

Good! I am here.
You are here, too.

Hap is here.

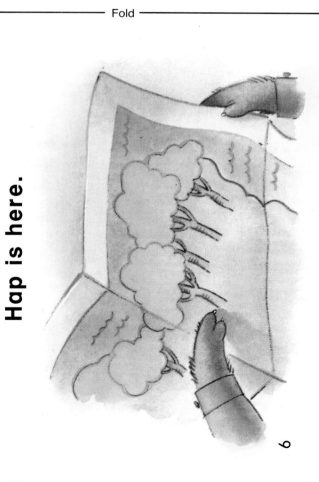

4

Read the map, Hap.
Read the map, Pam.

2

Where is Pam?

Fold

Harcourt

Fold

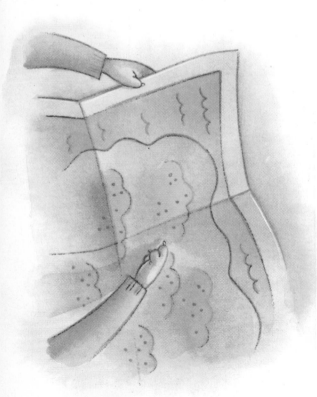

Pam is here.

5

Come here, Hap.
Come here, Pam.

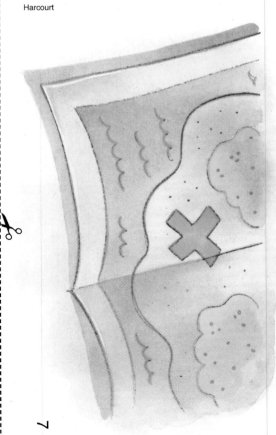

7

What Sam Did

See it, Sam?
It is brown.

Fold

Harcourt

Fold

Sam did come sit!

Come, Sam!

Together Again: Theme 2
Cut-out Fold-up Book

Sam went walking.

Fold

4

Come, Sam.
Sam did come.

Fold

Did Sam come?

4

Sit, Sam.

5

Get a Sack

Harcourt

— Fold —

What is in it?

8

— Fold —

Dan is going.
Dan has a big
sack, too.

3

Nan is going.
Nan has little
sacks.

9

4

Pam is going.
Pam has a green sack.

2

Kim is going.
Kim has a big sack.

Harcourt

Fold

Fold

Pam has a dog.
He has a sack, too.

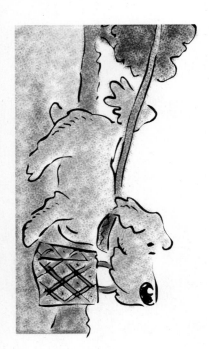

5

I see the sacks.
Pick a sack.

7

Come, Pals!

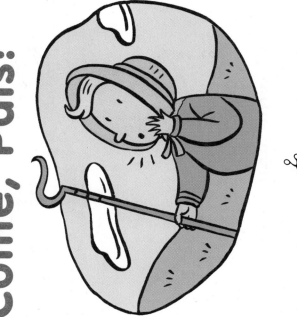

1

I call again.
"Come help me, pals!"

3

Harcourt

I am small.
I have a big call.

8

Three came down.
I call again.

6

4

One came down.
I call again.

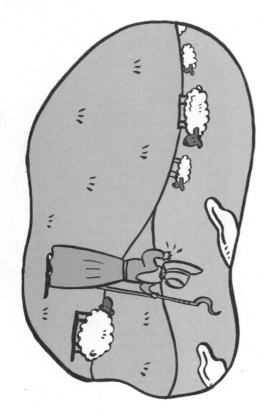

2

I call up the hill.
"I want you, pals!"

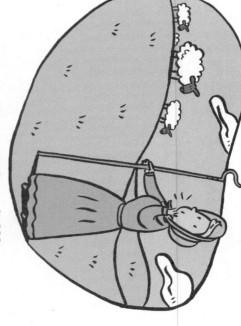

Fold

Harcourt

Fold

Two came down.
I call again.

5

"Come all!
Come down to me, pals!"

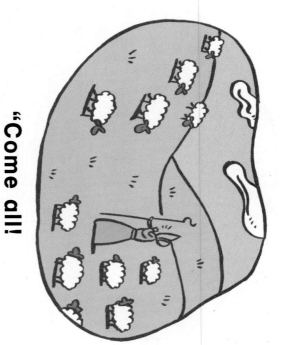

7

Join In

Name _____

▶ **Look at each picture. Circle the word that completes each sentence. Then write the word.**

sacks   docks   socks

_____

- - - - - - - - - - - - - - - - -

1. The _____ are on the mat.

cot   kit   cost

_____

- - - - - - - - - - - - - - - - -

2. The dolls are on the _____.

tip   tot   top

_____

- - - - - - - - - - - - - - - - -

3. The caps are on _____.

pats   pots   pond

_____

- - - - - - - - - - - - - - - - -

4. The lids are on the _____.

SCHOOL-HOME CONNECTION Ask your child to read the words he or she wrote. Look for things in the house whose names have the same short *o* vowel sound.

Harcourt

Name _____

▶ **Join the naming parts of the two sentences. Use the word <u>and</u>. Write the new sentence.**

1. Todd looked. Dog looked.

_____

_ _ _ _ _ _ _ _ _ _ _ _ _ _ _ _ _ _

_____

_ _ _ _ _ _ _ _ _ _ _ _ _ _ _ _ _ _

_____

2. Todd slid down. Dog slid down.

_____

_ _ _ _ _ _ _ _ _ _ _ _ _ _ _ _ _ _

_____

_ _ _ _ _ _ _ _ _ _ _ _ _ _ _ _ _ _

_____

TRY THIS Write two sentences about something you and a friend do together. Use the word <u>and</u> to join the naming parts of the two sentences.

SCHOOL-HOME CONNECTION Encourage your child to tell you about sentences that have two naming parts. Together, say some sentences about two family members or friends.

Harcourt

▶ **Write the word from the box that best completes each sentence.**

happy	They	my	was

_____

- - - - - - - - - - -

1. Hal and Ann came to _____ picnic.

_____

- - - - - - - - - - -

2. _____ sat with me.

_____

- - - - - - - - - - -

3. I am _____ that they came.

_____

- - - - - - - - - - -

4. It _____ hot.

SCHOOL-HOME CONNECTION Ask your child to read aloud the words in the box. Take turns making up sentences using those words.

Harcourt

Name _____

▶ **Write the word from the box that best completes each sentence.**

| this | forgot | day | Thank | so |

_____

5. Hal _____ his hat.

_____

6. Look at _____ hat!

_____

7. This hat is _____ big!

_____

8. Hal said, "_____ you."

_____

9. It was a happy _____.

TRY THIS Use some of the vocabulary words to write your own sentence about a picnic. Draw a picture to go with it.

Harcourt

▶ **Say the name of each picture.**
Color the picture if the name has the sound /o/.

1.

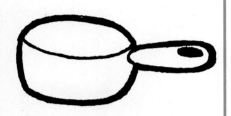

2.

3.

4.

5.

6.

7.

8.

9.

SCHOOL-HOME CONNECTION Find objects in the house whose names have the short *o* sound as in *hop*. Let your child hop from one short *o* object to the next.

Harcourt

▶ **In the story, Gil is happy at the
beginning. In the middle, he is sad. Then at
the end, he is very happy. Write below to tell why.**

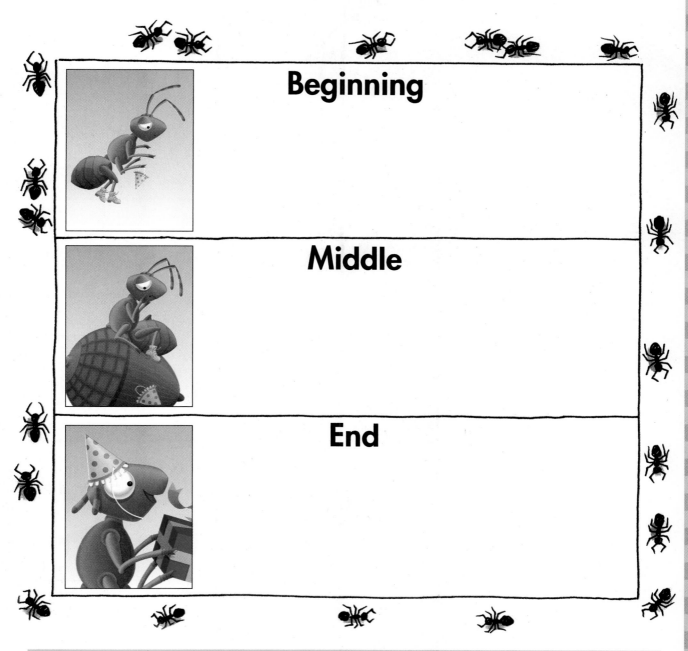

Beginning

Middle

End

TRY THIS What do you think will happen next to Gil and his
friends? Draw a picture to show your idea.

 SCHOOL-HOME CONNECTION Think of another story you and
your child know that has a happy ending. Tell it to one another.

Join In
Lesson 2

7

▶ **Say the name of the picture. Write <u>th</u>
if its name begins or ends with <u>th</u>.**

1. _th_

2. _____

3. _____

4. _____

5. _____

6. _____

7. _____

8. _____

9. _____

Harcourt

SCHOOL-HOME CONNECTION Sing together "Where Is
Thumbkin?" Encourage your child to add motions by wiggling
his or her thumbs as if they are talking to each other.

▶ **Look at each picture. Write the word from the box that completes each sentence.**

This	thin	path	moth	math

1. The cat hops on the _____ _ _ _ _ _ _ _ _ _ _ _ _ _ _ _ _____.

2.  Tom is good at _____ _ _ _ _ _ _ _ _ _ _ _ _ _ _ _____.

3.  Samson looks too _____ _ _ _ _ _ _ _ _ _ _ _ _ _ _____.

4. Can you see the _____ _ _ _ _ _ _ _ _ _ _ _ _ _ _ _ _____?

5.  _____ _ _ _ _ _ _ _ _ _ _ _ _____ hat looks good on me.

 **SCHOOL-HOME CONNECTION** Say the following words and ask your child to say a rhyming word that begins with the /th/ sound: *tank* (thank), *hum* (thumb), *horn* (thorn), and *tick* (thick).

Harcourt

Name _____

▶ **Read the clues. Write the word from the box that answers each riddle.**

| dog | ant | frog | cat |

1. I am black.

I am little.

What am I?

_____

- - - - - - - - - - - - - - - - -

_____

2. I am yellow.

I can run.

What am I?

_____

- - - - - - - - - - - - - - - - -

_____

3. I nap a lot.

You can pet me.

What am I?

_____

- - - - - - - - - - - - - - - - -

_____

4. I am green.

I can hop.

What am I?

_____

- - - - - - - - - - - - - - - - -

_____

SCHOOL-HOME CONNECTION Work with your child to make up a riddle. Ask another family member to solve the riddle.

Harcourt

Name _____

► **Name each picture. Listen to the beginning sounds. Write the two letters that stand for the beginning sounds.**

sk	sl	sn	sp	st

1. _____

2. _____

3. _____

4. _____

5. _____

6. _____

7. _____

8. _____

9. _____

SCHOOL-HOME CONNECTION Write the word *stop* and let your child read it aloud. Then have your child make a red stop sign.

Join In
Lesson 5

11

Harcourt

Name _____

▶ **Say the name of the picture. Write g if the name begins with g.**

1. _____

2. _g_

3. _____

4. _____

5. _____

6. _____

7. _____

8. _____

9. _____

SCHOOL-HOME CONNECTION Finish this sentence to plan a silly garden: *In my garden, I will grow....* Grow anything whose name begins with the sound of *g*.

Harcourt

▶ **Write the telling part of each sentence.**

1. Zack slid.

_____

- - - - - - - - - - - - - - - -

_____

2. Zack looks.

_____

- - - - - - - - - - - - - - - -

_____

3. He sees.

_____

- - - - - - - - - - - - - - - -

_____

4. He calls.

_____

- - - - - - - - - - - - - - - -

_____

5. I missed you, Mom.

_____

- - - - - - - - - - - - - - - -

_____

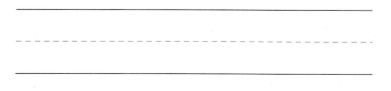

SCHOOL-HOME CONNECTION Encourage your child to say several sentences telling what he or she likes to do at home. Together, talk about the telling parts of your child's sentences.

Join In
Lesson 6

13

Harcourt

▶ **Write the word from the box that best completes each sentence.**

| go | like | better | time |

1. I _____ my bike.

2. I want to _____ on this bike.

3. It is _____ to go with a friend.

4. We have a good _____.

TRY THIS Write a sentence and then draw a picture about one thing you like to do. Use the word <u>like</u> in your writing.

SCHOOL-HOME CONNECTION Ask your child to read the word *like*. Talk about things your child likes to do. Plan to do one of the things together.

Harcourt

Name _____

▶ **Write a word to complete each sentence.**
Write one letter in each box.

_____

- - - - - - - - - - - - - - - - - -

1. They _____ going to the big house.

_____

- - - - - - - - - - - - - - - - - -

2. They like to go, _____ it is hot!

_____

- - - - - - - - - - - - - - - - - -

3. _____, they want to stop.

_____

- - - - - - - - - - - - - - - - - -

4. _____ happy now!

SCHOOL-HOME CONNECTION Ask your child to point to the
contraction I'*m*. Have him or her tell the two words that it stands for
and name the mark that shows a letter is missing.

Join In
Lesson 7   **15**

Harcourt

Phonics
Short Vowel: /o/o,
Consonant: /g/g

▶ **Read the story. Circle the words that begin with <u>G</u> or <u>g</u>. Underline the words that have the /o/ sound.**

Lost Dog

One day my dog Gil got lost. "Here, Gil!" I called. Gil did not come. Gil was not in the hall. "Are you up, Gil?" I called. "There you are!" Gil had a good nap. "Oh, Gil!" I said. "Let's go."

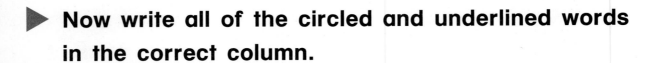

▶ **Now write all of the circled and underlined words in the correct column.**

g	o
1. _____	_____
2. _____	_____
3. _____	_____
4. _____	_____

SCHOOL-HOME CONNECTION Hide a stuffed toy. As your child looks for it, give clues by saying *Good* when he or she gets close and *Not good* when he or she gets farther away. Take turns hiding and finding the toy.

Name _____

▶ **Think about the story and write
what happened.**

In the beginning

In the middle

At the end

SCHOOL-HOME CONNECTION Ask your child to describe what is
happening in each picture. Then discuss his or her favorite part of
the story.

Join In
Lesson 7 **17**

Harcourt

▶ **Look at each picture. Circle the word that completes each sentence. Then write the word.**

Mom   Todd   Dad

1. This is _____.

---

moss   mitt   toss

2. He has my _____.

Todd   Ann   Dad

3. I am _____.

---

miss   add   mitt

4. I _____ it.

---

pan   pass   mitt

5. Will he _____ it to me?

TRY THIS Draw a picture of something or someone you miss. Write a sentence to go with your picture.

SCHOOL-HOME CONNECTION Read aloud the words your child added to the sentences on this page. Ask your child to clap twice after each word to remember the double consonant.

Harcourt

▶ **Look at each picture. Write the word that best completes the sentence.**

mitt	toss	Ann	add	pass

1. I am _____.

2. This is my _____.

3. I can _____ the ball.

4. I will _____ the bag.

5. I can _____ up the hits!

 **TRY THIS** What can you pass to someone else? Draw a picture of it. Write a sentence to go with your picture.

 SCHOOL-HOME CONNECTION Have your child read aloud one of the sentences he or she finished on this page. Ask your child to point out the double letters in the word he or she added.

Join In
Lesson 9   19

Harcourt

Name _____

▶ **Read the clue. Write the word that best
completes each sentence. Tell how you know.**

a day	a pet	a lock	a box

1. A cat can be one.
   A dog can be one, too.
   So can a bird.
   _____

   It is _____ .

   _____

   I know that _____ .

2. You can put things in it.
   You can get into a big one.
   It can have a top.
   _____

   It is _____ .

   _____

   I know that _____

   _____ .

SCHOOL-HOME CONNECTION Discuss this page with
your child. Ask whether he or she used the clues and/or
personal experiences to complete each sentence.

Harcourt

Name _____

▶ **Write the word that best completes each sentence.**

hops   hopped   hopping

_____

- - - - - - - - - - - - - - - - - -

1. The cats _____ down the path.

sits   sat   sitting

_____

- - - - - - - - - - - - - - - - - -

2. A dog was _____ on a log.

stops   stopped   stopping

_____

- - - - - - - - - - - - - - - - - -

3. The cats saw the dog and _____.

tip   tipped   tipping

_____

- - - - - - - - - - - - - - - - - -

4. The dog _____ his hat to the cats.

hop   hopped   hopping

_____

- - - - - - - - - - - - - - - - - -

5. They are all _____ down the path.

Harcourt

SCHOOL-HOME CONNECTION Work together to make a
list of the words with *-ed* and *-ing* that you used. Circle
any words where you doubled the final consonant.

Name _____

▶ **Use words from the box to complete the rhyme.**

hang	sang	song	long

_____

- - - - - - - - - - - - - - -

I _____ for my dad.

_____

- - - - - - - - - - - - - - -

It was a good _____ .

_____

- - - - - - - - - - - - - - -

Now I'll _____ up my socks,

_____

- - - - - - - - - - - - - - -

And I'll say, "So _____ ."

 TRY THIS Draw a picture of yourself helping out at home. Sing your favorite song softly as you draw.

SCHOOL-HOME CONNECTION Ask your child to help you with a household chore. Sing a song together while you work.

Harcourt

▶ **Say the name of the picture. Write <u>r</u> if the name begins with <u>r</u>.**

1. _____ r _____

2. _____

3. _____

4. _____

5. _____

6. _____

7. _____

8. _____

9. _____

TRY THIS Draw a picture of a rocket. What would you take with you if you flew in a rocket?

SCHOOL-HOME CONNECTION With your child, search through the house for things that are red. Say, "R-r-r-r," each time you find one.

Harcourt

▶ **Use _and_ to join the telling parts of the two sentences. Write the new sentence.**

I. Pam ran. Pam called the dog.

_____

- - - - - - - - - - - - - - - - - - -

_____

- - - - - - - - - - - - - - - - - - -

_____

2. Tip got up. Tip ran.

_____

- - - - - - - - - - - - - - - - - - -

_____

- - - - - - - - - - - - - - - - - - -

_____

 TRY THIS Can you do two things at the same time? Write a sentence about what you can do. Draw a picture to go with it.

SCHOOL-HOME CONNECTION With your child, talk about outdoor activities your family enjoys. Use some sentences with telling parts for two things people do.

Harcourt

Name _____

▶ **Write the word that best completes each sentence.**

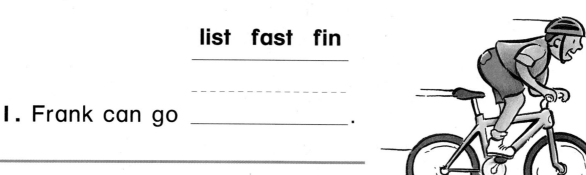

list   fast   fin

_____

- - - - - - - - - - - - -

1. Frank can go _____ .

fan   fit   for

_____

- - - - - - - - - - - - -

2. He can go _____ a long time.

at   off   one

_____

- - - - - - - - - - - - -

3. Did Frank get _____ his bike?

fall   hall   fan

_____

- - - - - - - - - - - - -

4. Did he _____?

if   stiff   staff

_____

- - - - - - - - - - - - -

5. Is his leg _____?

SCHOOL-HOME CONNECTION Practice saying this tongue twister with your child: *The first leaf fell off Friday.* Then ask your child to say other words that begin with the sound you hear at the beginning of *fall.*

Join In
Lesson 13   **29**

Name _____

▶ **Look at each picture. Write the word from the box that best completes each sentence about the picture.**

fin	fist	fast	fall	stiff	off

_____
- - - - - - - - - - - - -

1. It has a big _____.

_____
- - - - - - - - - - - - -

2. It can go _____.

_____
- - - - - - - - - - - - -

3. They will come _____.

_____
- - - - - - - - - - - - -

4. This is my _____.

_____
- - - - - - - - - - - - -

5. It is _____.

_____
- - - - - - - - - - - - -

6. They will _____.

Harcourt

SCHOOL-HOME CONNECTION Ask your child to read the words in the box and point out the words that end with the sound you hear at the end of *leaf*. Together, think of other words that end with the *f* sound.

Name _____

▶ **Name each picture. Listen to the beginning sounds. Write the two letters that stand for the beginning sound.**

| tr | cr | pr | dr | gr | fr |

1. _____

2. _____

3. _____

4. _____

5. _____

6. _____

7. _____

8. _____

9. _____

SCHOOL-HOME CONNECTION Ask your child to tell you about the pictures on this page. Together, think of other words that begin with the same sounds you hear at the beginning of the word *train*.

Join In
Lesson 15   **31**

Name _____

▶ **Write the words where they belong in the puzzles.**

bag   crab   bat   ball   crib   cab   bill

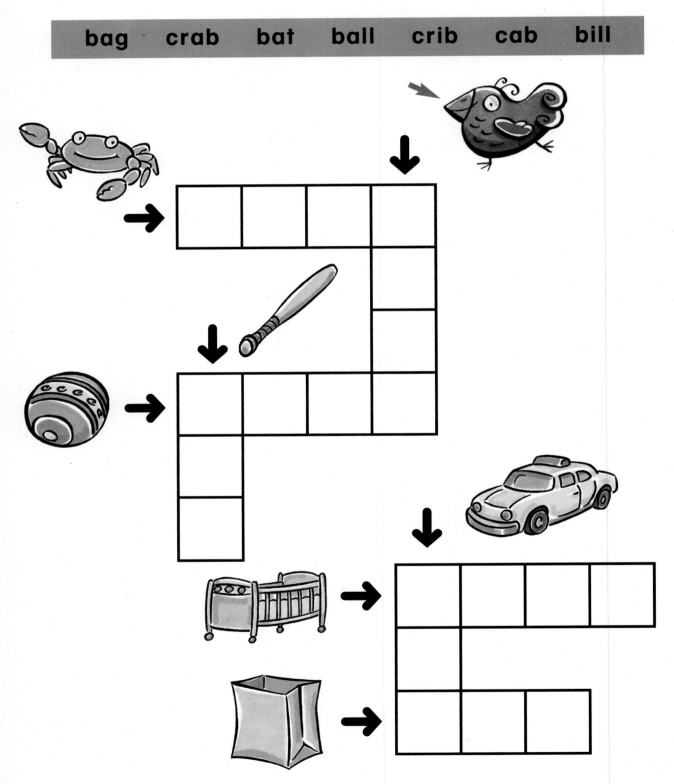

Join In
Lesson 16

SCHOOL-HOME CONNECTION Ask your child to name some of the pictures. Then have your child practice writing the letter b.

Harcourt

Name _____

▶ **Complete each sentence. Write
either a naming part or a telling part.**

_____
- - - - - - - - - - - - - - - - - - - -
1. Rabbits _____ .

_____
- - - - - - - - - - - - - - - - - - - -
2. _____ can hop.

_____
- - - - - - - - - - - - - - - - - - - -
3. Will and I _____ .

_____
- - - - - - - - - - - - - - - - - - - -
4. _____ played.

_____
- - - - - - - - - - - - - - - - - - - -
5. _____ is happy.

TRY THIS What else can you do? Write a complete sentence
telling about it. If you want, draw a picture to go
with your sentence.

SCHOOL-HOME CONNECTION Ask your child to say a complete
sentence, telling what he or she did today. Encourage your child
to write the sentence.

Harcourt

Name _____

▶ **Read the words in the box. Write the word that best completes each sentence.**

out	soon	Do	home	their

_____

1. _____ you see Bill and Mill?

_____

2. This is their _____ .

_____

3. Mill sits in _____ nest.

_____

4. Bill will go _____ .

_____

5. He comes back _____ .

SCHOOL-HOME CONNECTION Write the words *Do* and *home* and ask your child to read the words. Then have him or her name six things to do at home.

Harcourt

Name _____

► **Write the word that completes each sentence.**

best   been
_____

- - - - - - - - - - - - - - - -

1. Tess has lost her _____ mitt.

for   find
_____

- - - - - - - - - - - - - - - -

2. Can you help her _____ it?

Could   Catch
_____

- - - - - - - - - - - - - - - -

3. _____ it be in this bag?

put   pig
_____

- - - - - - - - - - - - - - - -

4. Did she _____ it in this box?

of   for
_____

- - - - - - - - - - - - - - - -

5. Look! Spot has it _____ her!

Harcourt

SCHOOL-HOME CONNECTION Write the words *best, find, could, put,* and *for* and ask your child to read them to you. Take turns making up sentences using each word.

Join In
Lesson 17   35

Name _____

Phonics

Consonants:
/b/b, /r/r
Short Vowel: /o/o

▶ **Look at each picture. Circle the word that completes the sentence. Then write the word.**

crab   crib   cab
_____

- - - - - - - - - - - - -

1. Bill was in the _____.

bid   tab   bib
_____

- - - - - - - - - - - - -

2. He had a big _____.

sob   cob   bat
_____

- - - - - - - - - - - - -

3. Why did Bill _____?

rib   bad   rob
_____

- - - - - - - - - - - - -

4.  Did the cat _____ him?

brick   bath   back
_____

- - - - - - - - - - - - -

5.  Bill was happy in the _____.

SCHOOL-HOME CONNECTION Ask your child to read one of the sentences he or she completed on this page. Together, think of names for people or pets that begin with the letter *B*.

Harcourt

Name _____

▶ **Think about the story. Draw what
happened first, next, and last.**

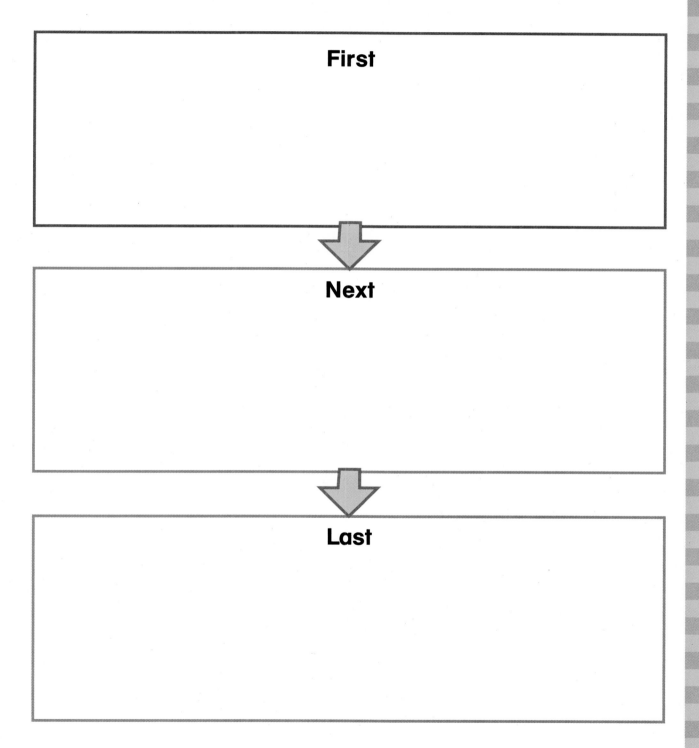

First

Next

Last

SCHOOL-HOME CONNECTION Ask your child to tell you the
beginning, the middle, and the end of the story. Ask what he or
she liked best about it.

Join In
Lesson 17   37

Harcourt

Name _____

▶ **Write the word from the box that names each picture.**

fort	corn	thorn	horn	fork	torn

1.

_____

- -

_____

2.

_____

- -

_____

3.

_____

- -

_____

4.

_____

- -

_____

5.

_____

- -

_____

6.

_____

- -

_____

TRY THIS Write your own sentence with the word <u>or</u>. Draw a picture to go with your sentence.

Join In
Lesson 18

38

SCHOOL-HOME CONNECTION Ask your child to write the word *or*. Then have your child say several other words that include the *or* sound.

Harcourt

Name _____

▶ **Finish the story. Write the word from the box that completes each sentence.**

Bob	for	corn	born

Mort's Pig

"I like your pig," said Ann.

_____

_____

"He was _____ on Monday," Mort said.

_____

_____

"I will call him _____."

Ann asked, "What is he eating?"

_____

_____

"That is _____," Mort said. "It is good

_____

_____

_____ pigs."

SCHOOL-HOME CONNECTION Ask your child to write the word *born*. Discuss the date on which he or she was born.

Join In
Lesson 19   **39**

Harcourt

Name _____

▶ **Look at the pictures. Write the word from the box that best completes each sentence.**

| masks | stork | stacks | sticks | spots |

_____

1. Where is the _____?

_____

2. I see two _____.

_____

3. The dog has three _____.

_____

4. I see two _____ of blocks.

_____

5. I see lots of _____.

TRY THIS Write a sentence about your favorite sport. Draw a picture to go with your sentence.

SCHOOL-HOME CONNECTION Ask your child to write the word *list*. You may want to say the word slowly to help your child write the letter that stands for each sound. Then have your child suggest other words that end with the *-st* sounds.

Harcourt

Name _____

▶ **Look at each picture. Circle the word that completes the sentence. Then write the word.**

1. My horse will _____.

drill
trot
trick

2. This _____ is tall.

grass
grin
drip

3. Can we _____ here?

crank
from
cross

4. The horses _____.

trim
drink
drip

TRY THIS Where would you like to go? Write your own sentence with the word <u>trip</u>. Draw a picture to go with your sentence.

SCHOOL-HOME CONNECTION Have your child read aloud one of the words he or she wrote on this page. Ask your child to say other words that begin with the same pair of letters as that word does.

Join In
Lesson 20   41

▶ **Look at each picture. Use a word from the box to complete each sentence.**

wag	wings	wick	wink	swim

1. It has a _____.

2. It has a tail to _____.

3. It can _____.

4. It has two _____.

5. It can _____.

TRY THIS Think of something to write a clue about. When you write your clue, use words that describe it.

SCHOOL-HOME CONNECTION Ask your child to read some of the words he or she wrote on this page. Then have your child practice writing the letter w.

Harcourt

Name _____

▶ **Choose the naming word that best completes each sentence.**

friend   fish

_____

- - - - - - - - - - - - - - - - - - -

1. I play with my _____.

snacks   socks

- - - - - - - - - - - - - - - - - -

2. We eat _____ first.

bill   ball

_____

- - - - - - - - - - - - - - - - - -

3. Then we toss the _____.

eyes   fish

_____

- - - - - - - - - - - - - - - - - -

4. We look for big _____.

SCHOOL-HOME CONNECTION Let your child share what he or she learned about naming words. Then ask your child to say the naming words for various people and things in your home.

Join In
Lesson 21

43

Harcourt

Name _____

▶ **Write the word that completes
each sentence.**

From   First

_____

- - - - - - - - - - - - - -

1. _____, we run down the hill.

fish   find

_____

- - - - - - - - - - - - - -

2. I try to catch a _____.

from   pushes

_____

- - - - - - - - - - - - - -

3. Now my dad _____ me
on this swing.

grow   first

_____

- - - - - - - - - - - - - -

4. Will I _____ big,
like my dad?

Harcourt

SCHOOL-HOME CONNECTION Talk with your child about what
the word *grow* means. Ask him or her to name things that grow.

first   from

_____

- - - - - - - - - - - - - - -

5. Where did the dog come _____?

does   first

_____

- - - - - - - - - - - - - - -

6. What _____ he see?

gone   grow

_____

- - - - - - - - - - - - - - -

7. The cat is _____!

 TRY THIS Make up a short story about the cat and the dog.
Draw a picture to go with it.

Harcourt

Name _____

Phonics

Consonants:
/w/w, /g/g
Digraph: /th/th

▶ **Write the words where they belong in the puzzle.**

| wing | gas | swing | think | wig | wag |

1.

2.

3.

4.

5.

6.

SCHOOL-HOME CONNECTION Encourage your child to share the crossword puzzle he or she completed by reading some of the words aloud. Then ask your child to say other words that begin with the letter *w*.

Harcourt

Name _____

▶ **Look at the chart and answer the
questions. Use what you learned in the story.**

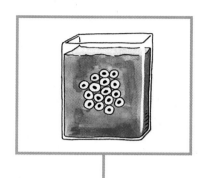

I. Where do frogs come from?

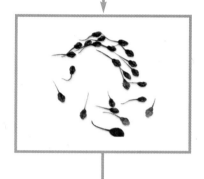

2. What are they called at first?

3. What do frogs grow?

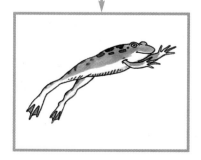

4. What do big frogs eat?

SCHOOL-HOME CONNECTION Ask your child what he or
she learned about frogs in this story. What else would he
or she like to know? Look it up at the library.

Join In
Lesson 22   47

Harcourt

Name _____

▶ **Write the word from the box that names each picture.**

| dish | ship | flash | shop | fish | shack |

1.

_____

- - - - - - - - - - - - - - -

_____

2.

_____

- - - - - - - - - - - - - - -

_____

3.

_____

- - - - - - - - - - - - - - -

_____

4.

_____

- - - - - - - - - - - - - - -

_____

5.

_____

- - - - - - - - - - - - - - -

_____

6.

_____

- - - - - - - - - - - - - - -

_____

TRY THIS Finish this sentence: I wish _____.

Draw a picture to go with your sentence.

SCHOOL-HOME CONNECTION Ask your child to write the word *fish*. Then have your child say several other words that include the /sh/ sound.

Harcourt

Name _____

▶ **Look at each picture. Circle the word that completes the sentence. Then write the word.**

_____

1. I _____ I were tall.

worn

wish

dash

_____

2. I am not _____.

shop

shock

short

_____

3. I want to eat _____.

corn

flash

fort

_____

4. I play the _____.

hand

cash

horn

_____

5. I want to play _____.

spots

sports

shots

TRY THIS Write your own sentence with the word <u>dish</u>. Draw a picture to go with your sentence.

SCHOOL-HOME CONNECTION Ask your child to read aloud one of the sentences he or she completed. Have your child point out the two letters that spell the /sh/ sound or the /ôr/ sound.

Harcourt

Name _____

▶ **Read the story. Then draw and label a picture that shows two details from the story.**

Cats

Cats are good pets. Cats like to run. They like to play. They like to get up on your bed. They like <u>you</u>! Go get a cat for a pet.

Join In
Lesson 24

SCHOOL-HOME CONNECTION As you read a book together, pause after some pages and ask your child to recall the most important fact or detail in that part of the story.

Harcourt

Name _____

► **Finish each sentence. Add <u>es</u> to the word above the line.**

splash

_____

- -

1. The fish _____.

dish

_____

- -

2. Look at the _____.

wish

_____

- -

3. Tim _____ for some help.

wash

_____

- -

4. Cass _____ her dog

on Monday.

TRY THIS Write your own sentence with the word <u>swishes.</u> Draw a picture to go with your sentence.

SCHOOL-HOME CONNECTION Have your child read aloud some of the words he or she wrote on this page. Together, think of other words ending with *sh* that take the ending *-es*.

Join In

Lesson 25   **51**

Harcourt

▶ **Complete each sentence. Write the contraction for the two words.**

 I   will
_____

- - - - - - - - - - - - - - - - - - - -

1. _____ go to the top now.

 Who   will
_____

- - - - - - - - - - - - - - - - - - - -

2. _____ come with me?

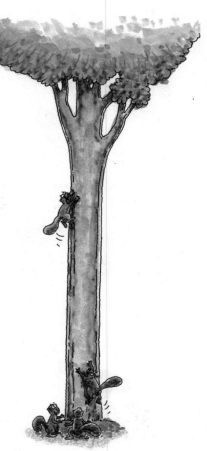

 You   will
_____

- - - - - - - - - - - - - - - - - - - -

3. _____ like it up here!

 He   will
_____

- - - - - - - - - - - - - - - - - - - -

4. _____ go up first.

 I   will
_____

- - - - - - - - - - - - - - - - - - - -

5. _____ see you at the top!

Harcourt

SCHOOL-HOME CONNECTION Ask your child to point out one of the contractions he or she wrote. Then have your child identify the two words that are combined in that contraction.

▶ **Write the word from the box that names each picture.**

| net | bell | pen | desk | bed | men | web | sled | ten |

1.

_____

- - - - - - - - -

_____

2.

_____

- - - - - - - - -

_____

3.

_____

- - - - - - - - -

_____

4.

_____

- - - - - - - - -

_____

5.

_____

- - - - - - - - -

_____

6.

_____

- - - - - - - - -

_____

7.

_____

- - - - - - - - -

_____

8.

_____

- - - - - - - - -

_____

9.

_____

- - - - - - - - -

_____

SCHOOL-HOME CONNECTION Use the words on this page to explore short vowel sounds. Substitute the *e* in each word with another vowel (*ten, tan*). Talk about the new words (or nonsense words) that are created.

Join In
Lesson 26   **53**

Harcourt

▶ **Look at each picture. Circle the word
that completes the sentence. Then write the word.**

want   went   sent

1. Greg _____ to the park.

met   bet   bat

2. He _____ Tess there.

pit   pat   pet

3. Tess had her new _____.

hem · hen   hint

4. It was a _____.

TRY THIS Write your own sentence with the word <u>let</u>. Draw a picture to go with your sentence.

SCHOOL-HOME CONNECTION Ask your child to name some of the pictures on page 53. Have your child point out the *e* in each word in the box on that page.

Harcourt

▶ **Write the words that name a person or a place in each sentence.**

1. Mother is on the hill.

_____   _____

- - - - - - - - - -   - - - - - - - - - -

_____   _____

2. Dad walks to the pond.

_____   _____

- - - - - - - - - -   - - - - - - - - - -

_____   _____

3. The girl has a doll.

_____

- - - - - - - - - -

_____

4. My sister got a pet at a shop.

_____   _____

- - - - - - - - - -   - - - - - - - - - -

_____   _____

5. The boys look together.

_____

- - - - - - - - - -

SCHOOL-HOME CONNECTION Ask your child to tell you about nouns that name places. Together, name places where your child likes to spend time.

Join In
Lesson 26   55

Harcourt

Name _____

▶ **Write the word that best completes each sentence.**

for   found   fox
_____

1. Look what I _____ .

---

wait   walk   will
_____

2. I can't _____ to pick it up.

---

noisy   need   not
_____

3. You _____ to see it.

---

when   where   white
_____

4. It is red and _____ .

Maybe   Miss   Make
_____

5. _____ you can help me.

56 Join In
Lesson 27

SCHOOL-HOME CONNECTION Ask your child to read
the words that were used to complete the sentences
and then to read the sentences aloud.

Harcourt

Name _____

▶ **Write the word that best completes each sentence.**

talk   take   time

_____

- - - - - - - - - - - - - - - -

1. I can _____ it out of the box.

---

ever   end   egg

_____

- - - - - - - - - - - - - - - -

2. It will be the best pet _____.

Note   No   New

_____

- - - - - - - - - - - - - - - -

3. _____ pet is better.

---

nice   nose   next

_____

- - - - - - - - - - - - - - - -

4. I will get one _____ time.

TRY THIS Think of a name for the puppy. Write a sentence telling why you think it is a good name. Try to use one of the Vocabulary Words in your sentence.

SCHOOL-HOME CONNECTION Ask your child to read the words used to complete the sentences and then to read the sentences aloud.

Join In
Lesson 27   **57**

Name _____

Phonics

Short Vowel: /e/e
Consonant: /w/w
Digraph: /sh/sh

▶ **Read each sentence. Add to the pictures.**

1.

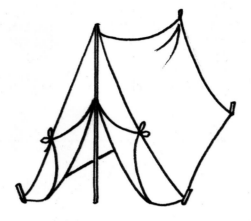

This tent is red.

2.

Now there are six shells.

3.

This web is wet.

4.

I am on the sled.

SCHOOL-HOME CONNECTION Encourage your child to share the pictures he or she has drawn. Ask your child how he or she knew what to draw.

Harcourt

► **Circle the sentences that tell what happens in the story. Then draw a picture to show what happens next.**

1. "I found an egg," said Daniel.

2. "I think an 🐦 is inside," said Daniel.

3. "I think an 🐊 will come out of it," said Meg.

4. "I think a 🦆 is going to come out," said Daniel.

5. The children waited and waited.

SCHOOL-HOME CONNECTION Have your child tell about the story characters in *Daniel's Mystery Egg*. Ask your child who his or her favorite character is and why.

Name _____

▶ **Write the word from the box that best completes each sentence.**

Fox	mix	box	Ox	six

_____

1. Help me _____ this snack.

_____

2. _____ will help me.

_____

3. It will fit in this _____.

_____

4. Happy Birthday, _____!

_____

5. My _____ pals can eat with me.

✎ **TRY THIS** Write your own sentence with the word <u>fix</u>. Draw a picture to go with your sentence.

SCHOOL-HOME CONNECTION Ask your child to spell the word *ox*. Then ask your child to say other words that have the /ks/ sound.

Harcourt

Help Me Get It

1

It was here.
Help me get it.

3

Harcourt

— Fold —

— Fold —

This was a good day!
We are happy at last.

8

Where is my cat?
I forgot where it is.

6

Where is my snack?
I think the dog has it.

Where is my pig?
It's so small and pink.

Stop, dog!
I want my snack!

The cat is on top of the box.
Now I see it.

Fold

Fold

Harcourt

What Can You Make?

Fold

Harcourt

Yes, I'm going to make a doll.

Fold

What can you make now?

8

What will Todd make this time?
Go to it, Todd.

6

This is what Nan has.
It is a lot!

I like to make things.
This is what I have.

Harcourt

Fold

Fold

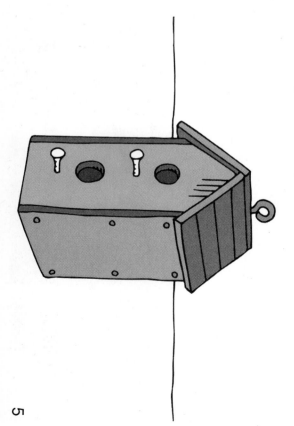

Nan makes a small house.

It looks better now.
Do you like what he did?

Too Many Fish

1

Fold

Harcourt

Fold

How did they get in here? What is
a way to get rid of six fish?

3

8

Help!

What is a better way?
I will think hard.

6

Little fish, come here.
Come this way.

2

Help! Six fish are in my bath.
That is too many fish.

Harcourt

Go fish, go! Go that way.
I do not want you in my bath. 7

Now I have three fish in my bath.
That is still too many fish!

5

Here Comes Dash

1

Kris and Will hop up and down, but Dash runs in.

3

Thank you, Dash.
I'm so glad you came!

8

Kris wants a snack.

6

Kris has a ball,
but Dash wants it, too!

Kris and Fran are happy,
but Dash pushes in.

— Fold —

— Fold —

Harcourt

Now, Kris has gone out.
Now, here comes Dash!

Kris runs to catch this.
Dash does, too!

Fix-It Fox

1

"Yes, my pet," said Fox.

3

"Now maybe you could fix me," said Fox.

8

"Fox!" cried Peg. "I am getting very wet! Take a look at this well."

6

Harcourt

Fold

Fold

"Fox!" cried Peg. "I need to rest. Will you fix the three legs on the bed?"

"Fox!" cried Peg. "This is a very big mess. Will you ever finish the shed?"

Harcourt

"I'll be there soon," said Fox. 7

"That's next," said Fox.

5

Special
Times

▶ **Circle the word that best completes the sentence. Write the word.**

stick
thick
chick

1. The _____ rips

his yellow hat.

Fat
Fetch
Fish

2. "_____ my pins,"

says Mom Hen.

patch
pan
pat

3. Mom Hen makes a small

_____.

stiff
stitch
sting

4. She will _____ it on.

skill
hill
chill

5. Now Chick will not get a

_____.

Harcourt

Name _____

▶ **Write the words in the barn that name animals. Write the words in the house that name things.**

worm   lamp   bed   pig   apple   cat   chick   bike

1. _____

2. _____

3. _____

4. _____

5. _____

6. _____

7. _____

8. _____

TRY THIS Draw a picture of an animal you like. Label the picture.

SCHOOL-HOME CONNECTION Look through a photo album or magazine with your child. Think of as many different words as you can to name each thing or animal.

Harcourt

► **Write the word that best completes each sentence.**

yard   yet   your

_____

- - - - - - - - - - - - - - - - -

1. Is _____ pet big?

for   feet   farm

_____

- - - - - - - - - - - - - - - - -

2. My pet has very big _____.

went   will   when

_____

- - - - - - - - - - - - - - - - -

3. One of my pals ran _____ he saw it.

over   other   off

_____

- - - - - - - - - - - - - - - - -

4. My _____ pal saw it, too.

Harcourt

Name _____

▶ **Write the word that best completes each sentence.**

hand   happy   hide

_____

- - - - - - - - - - - - - - - - -

1. My pals _____

when they see it.

2. Did you see my pet walk

but   by   both

_____

- - - - - - - - - - - - - - - - -

_____ ?

mop   man   much

_____

- - - - - - - - - - - - - - - - -

3. I like my pet very _____ .

 TRY THIS Draw the best pet you can imagine. Write three words to describe it.

SCHOOL-HOME CONNECTION Ask your child to read the words that were used to complete the sentences and then read the sentences aloud.

Special Times
Lesson 2   **5**

Harcourt

▶ **Circle the sentence that tells about each picture.**

1. Chip likes to chop the ball.
   Chip likes to pitch the ball.
   Chip likes to sketch the ball.

2. Rich can not catch the ball.
   Rich can catch the ball.
   Rich chats with Chip.

3. The friends play hopscotch.
   The friends hop in the ditch.
   The friends sit on a bench.

4. Wag can hatch a chick.
   Wag can get on the branch.
   Wag can fetch the stick.

5. Chet is the champ.
   Chet chomps on an apple.
   Chet checks the chimp.

SCHOOL-HOME CONNECTION Watch part of a sports game together. Talk about the rules. Ask your child to draw a picture of a sports champion.

Harcourt

Name _____

▶ **Think about the story. Look at the pictures and write what happened next.**

They saw how big he was.

THEN

_____

- - - - - - - - - - - - - - - - - - - -

_____

She said, "Catch me if you can!"

THEN

_____

- - - - - - - - - - - - - - - - - - - -

_____

He got her!

THEN

_____

- - - - - - - - - - - - - - - - - - - -

_____

Harcourt

SCHOOL-HOME CONNECTION Ask your child to use the pictures
and sentences to tell you the story "Catch Me If You Can!"

Special Times
Lesson 2   7

▶ **Write the word from the box that names each picture.**

| candle | rattle | pickle | apple | bottle | kettle |

1.

_____

- - - - - - - - - - - -

_____

2.

_____

- - - - - - - - - - - -

_____

3.

_____

- - - - - - - - - - - -

_____

4.

_____

- - - - - - - - - - - -

_____

5.

_____

- - - - - - - - - - - -

_____

6.

_____

- - - - - - - - - - - -

_____

SCHOOL–HOME CONNECTION Say these words that end in *le*: *wiggle, giggle, cackle, paddle, tickle.* Let your child act out the words.

Harcourt

Name _____

▶ **Read the riddles. Choose the best answer and write it on the line.**

1. Ducks do it when they walk.

Is it **waddle**, **rattle**, or **wall**?

_____

- - - - - - - - - - - - - - - - - -

_____

2. You do it if you are happy.

Is it **giggle**, **good**, or **grill**?

_____

- - - - - - - - - - - - - - - - - -

_____

3. It is not big.

Is it **let**, **list**, or **little**?

_____

- - - - - - - - - - - - - - - - - -

_____

4. It makes a good snack.

Is it **again**, **apple**, or **all**?

_____

- - - - - - - - - - - - - - - - - -

_____

5. You can make something to eat in it.

Is it **cackle**, **kettle**, or **kid**?

_____

- - - - - - - - - - - - - - - - - -

_____

6. You can put this in a sandwich.

Is it **play**, **pickle**, or **pimple**?

_____

- - - - - - - - - - - - - - - - - -

_____

Harcourt

SCHOOL-HOME CONNECTION Ask your child to read each riddle to family members and challenge them to guess the answers.

Name _____

▶ **Look at the dinosaurs. Write <u>real</u> or <u>not real</u> under each one.**

1.

_____

- - - - - - - - - - - - - - -

_____

2.

_____

- - - - - - - - - - - - - - -

_____

3.

_____

- - - - - - - - - - - - - - -

_____

4.

_____

- - - - - - - - - - - - - - -

_____

5.

_____

- - - - - - - - - - - - - - -

_____

6.

_____

- - - - - - - - - - - - - - -

_____

TRY THIS Draw your own picture of a dinosaur doing something, and label it <u>real</u> or <u>not real</u>.

SCHOOL-HOME CONNECTION Have your child describe what he or she sees in each picture.

Harcourt

Name _____

▶ **Write cl, fl, or pl to complete each word.**

_____
- - - - - - - - - - -
1. Milt can do a _____ip.

_____
- - - - - - - - - - -
2. Milt has a _____ant.

_____
- - - - - - - - - - -
3. A _____ag pops out.

_____
- - - - - - - - - - -
4. It's a _____ock.

_____
- - - - - - - - - - -
5. We giggle and _____ap.

TRY THIS Draw a clown doing a funny trick. Write a title for your picture.

SCHOOL-HOME CONNECTION Ask your child to read the sentences to you. Work together to think of more words that begin with the same sounds as *plant*, *flag*, and *clock*.

Harcourt

Name _____

▶ **Name each picture. Write _ar_ if the name has _ar_ in it.**

1. c_____

2. c_____d

3. c_____n

4. sc_____f

5. h_____se

6. h_____p

7. h_____n

8. st_____

9. b_____n

TRY THIS Make a greeting card. Give it to a friend or family member.

SCHOOL-HOME CONNECTION The next time you take a ride in a car, make a game of naming as many *ar* words as you can.

Harcourt

Name _____

▶ **Write the word that best completes each sentence.**

pal   pals

_____

- - - - - - - - - - - - - -

1. The two _____ go shopping.

ball   balls

_____

- - - - - - - - - - - - - -

2. They get a bat and a _____.

hat   hats

_____

- - - - - - - - - - - - - -

3. They get two _____.

girl   girls

_____

- - - - - - - - - - - - - -

4. One _____ wants a snack.

apple   apples

_____

- - - - - - - - - - - - - -

5. They get some red _____ to eat.

SCHOOL-HOME CONNECTION Let your child help you make a shopping list. Ask which words on the list name more than one.

Special Times
Lesson 6   **13**

Harcourt

▶ **Write the word that best completes each sentence.**

when   week   yet

_____

1. I'm glad this _____ is over!

Nothing   Nap   Then

_____

2. _____ went right.

sister   some   made

_____

3. First, my _____ drops my ant farm.

Every   Egg   Are

_____

4. _____ ant came out!

some   soon   pushes

_____

5. I think _____ got in my bed.

other   yet   yell

_____

- -

6. It was not _____ time for bed, when it fell.

right   rip   every

_____

- -

7. It crashed _____ off my desk.

nothing   made   much

_____

- - - - - - - - - - - - - - - - - -

8. Mom said, "This _____ a mess!"

turned   tell   told

_____

- - - - - - - - - - - - - - - - -

9. Next, I _____ on the TV.

walk   watch   what

_____

- - - - - - - - - - - - - - - -

10. When I started to _____ it, it broke.

SCHOOL-HOME CONNECTION Write the word *week* and let your child read it to you. Use a calendar to help your child name the days of the week.

Harcourt

▶ **Read the word. Circle the pictures whose names have the same vowel sound.**

1. start

2. dark

3. hard

▶ **Read the sentences. Write the word that best completes each one.**

farm   form

_____

- -

4. The _____ is small.

_____

barn   bark

_____

- -

5. Sam found a chick in the _____ .

_____

card   car

_____

- -

6. The dog barks at the _____ .

SCHOOL-HOME CONNECTION Talk with your child about the jobs of people you know. Discuss when people start their workday.

Harcourt

▶ **Circle the sentence that tells about each picture.**

1. The little dog yips and yaps.
   Yes, that is a yak.
   The dog is yellow.

2. The kids yell in the barn.
   The kids have some yarn.
   The kids play in the yard.

3. Tim pushes the yarn fast.
   Tim has a yellow hat on.
   Tim did not put his hat on yet.

4. "Will you plant this yam?" said Mom.
   "This gift is for you," said Mom.
   "This yard is for you," said Mom.

5. The big dogs yelp.
   The fans are not here yet.
   The happy fans yell.

TRY THIS Draw a picture or design. Use only your yellow crayon and one other color.

SCHOOL-HOME CONNECTION Say word pairs like *wet/yet, yes/less, yap/rap,* and *fell/yell.* Ask your child to say *yes* when you say a word that begins with *y.*

Special Times
Lesson 9   **19**

Harcourt

Name _____

▶ **Put together the word and the word ending above the line. Write the new word on the line.**

look + ed

_____

- - - - - - - - - - - - - - - -

1. Nick _____ at all the stars.

want + s

_____

- - - - - - - - - - - - - - - -

2. He _____ a big red star.

paint + ing

_____

- - - - - - - - - - - - - - - -

3. I am _____ a red star.

get + s

_____

- - - - - - - - - - - - - - - -

4. Nick _____ a star.

TRY THIS Write your own sentence about Nick. Use the word <u>shout</u>, and add the ending <u>ed</u>.

SCHOOL-HOME CONNECTION Ask your child to choose one of the sentences on this page and read it aloud. Discuss the ending added to the verb.

Harcourt

▶ **Read the story. Then finish the sentences.**

A Little Horse Is Born

One morning a little horse was born on our farm. The little horse was not in the barn. It was in the yard by a stack of corn. Dad got me up to see it. I grabbed my yarn hat and ran to the yard.

I watched the little horse get up. It made one step and then another. The mother led it to the barn.

1. A little horse was

_____

- - - - - - - - - - - - - -

_____ .

2. It was by a stack of

_____

- - - - - - - - - - - - - -

_____ .

3. I grabbed my

_____

- - - - - - - - - - - - - -

_____ hat.

4. The little horse was led

_____

- - - - - - - - - - - - - -

to the _____ .

SCHOOL-HOME CONNECTION Ask your child to draw what he or she probably looked like as a newborn baby. If you have baby pictures, look at them together.

Special Times
Lesson 10   **21**

Harcourt

Name _____

▶ **Name each picture. Write the word from the box.**

| duck | bug | cup | truck | skunk | bus |

1. _____
_____

2. _____
_____

3. _____
_____

4. _____
_____

5. _____
_____

6. _____
_____

SCHOOL-HOME CONNECTION Start with the word *bug*. Take turns replacing the initial or final letters to create more short *u* words.

Harcourt

Name _____

▶ **Write the special names and special titles correctly.**

1. bud dunn

_____

- - - - - - - - - - - - - - - - - - - -

_____

- - - - - - - - - - - - - - - - - - - -

2. uncle chuck _____

_____

- - - - - - - - - - - - - - - - - - - -

3. mrs. dunn _____

_____

- - - - - - - - - - - - - - - - - - - -

4. dr. duff _____

_____

- - - - - - - - - - - - - - - - - - - -

5. russ _____

_____

- - - - - - - - - - - - - - - - - - - -

6. mr. huff _____

Harcourt

SCHOOL-HOME CONNECTION Help your child make a list of people he or she knows. Make sure all the names and titles begin with a capital letter.

Special Times
Lesson 11   **23**

Name _____

▶ **Write the word from the box that best completes each sentence.**

about	any	why	always

1. I _____ fish with Tim.

2. Tell us _____ this lake.

3. Are there _____ fish here?

4. Do you know _____ I always catch big ones?

SCHOOL-HOME CONNECTION Ask your child to point to each word in the box, say the word, and use it in a sentence.

Harcourt

Name _____

▶ **Draw pictures to show what frightened each person in the story.**

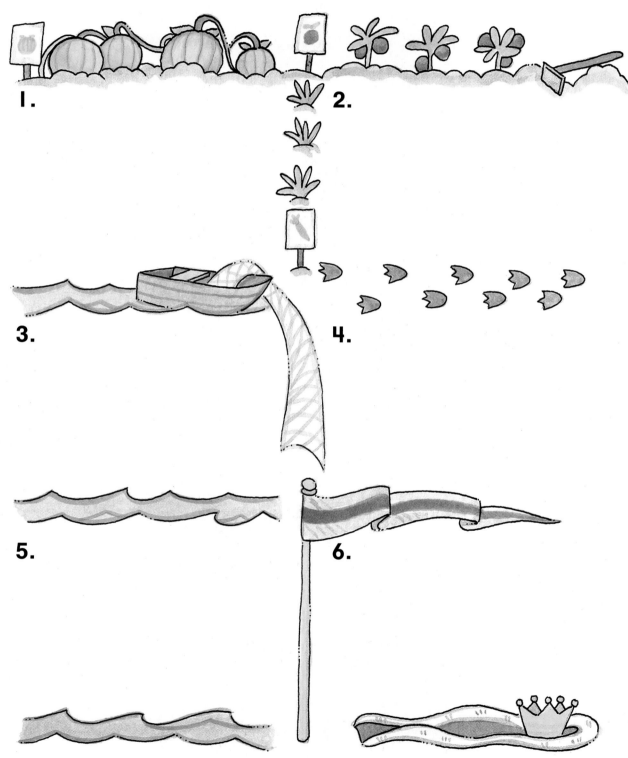

1.

2.

3.

4.

5.

6.

SCHOOL-HOME CONNECTION Ask your child to use the drawings to retell the story *Too Much Talk*.

Special Times
Lesson 12   27

Harcourt

Name _____

Phonics

Consonants: /j/j,
/z/z, zz,
Digraph: /kw/qu

▶ **Read the word. Circle the pictures whose names have the same beginning sound.**

1. jazz

2. zip

3. quit

▶ **Read the sentences. Write the word that best completes each one.**

puzzle   juggle

_____

- - - - - - - - - - - - - - - - - -

4. Have you seen this _____?

quit   quick

_____

- - - - - - - - - - - - - - - - - -

5. The fish is so _____.

jug   just

_____

- - - - - - - - - - - - - - - - - -

6. I got there _____ in time.

SCHOOL-HOME CONNECTION Say some words that have the sound of z and some that do not. Let your child make a buzzing sound whenever he or she hears the z sound.

Harcourt

Name _____

Phonics
Consonants: /j/j,
/z/z, zz,
Digraph: /kw/qu

▶ **Write the word from the box that best completes each sentence.**

| jump | Zeb | quit | job | quick | jazz |

1. _____ has a horn.

2. He likes _____.

3. He does a good _____.

4. His songs are so _____!

5. They make us want to _____.

6. We don't want him to _____.

SCHOOL-HOME CONNECTION Listen to music with your child. Find a fast song and then jump and jig together.

Special Times
Lesson 14

29

Harcourt

Name _____

▶ **Write words to finish each sentence.**
Draw a picture for each sentence.

REAL

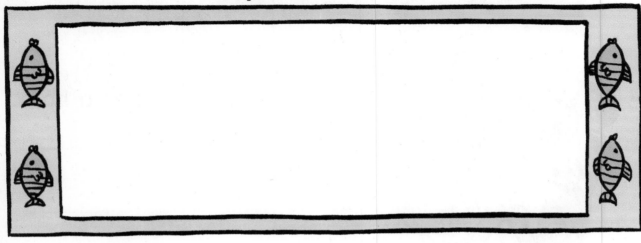

The dog can _____ .

NOT REAL

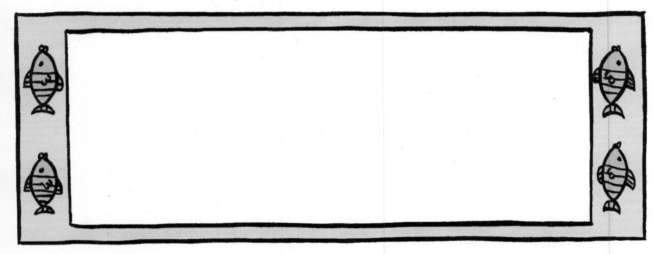

The dog and I will _____ .

Special Times
Lesson 14

SCHOOL-HOME CONNECTION Have your child make up a story to go with each drawing. Talk with your child about what is real and what is make-believe.

Harcourt

Name _____

Write the word from the box that names each picture.

| blocks | clap | flag | plant | plum | sled |

1.

_____

- - - - - - - - - - - - - - -

_____

2.

_____

- - - - - - - - - - - - - - -

_____

3.

_____

- - - - - - - - - - - - - - -

_____

4.

_____

- - - - - - - - - - - - - - -

_____

5.

_____

- - - - - - - - - - - - - - -

_____

6.

_____

- - - - - - - - - - - - - - -

_____

SCHOOL-HOME CONNECTION Ask your child to choose one of the pictures on this page and read the word that names the picture. Together, think of other words that begin with the same sounds.

Special Times
Lesson 15   31

▶ **Write a word from the box to complete each sentence.**

| stump | camp | Gramps | plump | tramp |

_____

1. _____ and I

look for animals.

_____

2. We _____ through

grass and trees.

3. We see a rabbit by an old tree

_____

_____ .

_____

4. We see a _____ robin.

_____

5. Then we _____ and eat lunch.

SCHOOL-HOME CONNECTION Start with the word *grump*.
Take turns replacing letters to create new words.

Harcourt

▶ **Say the name of each picture. Color
the pictures with names that begin with <u>v</u>.**

TRY THIS Where would you like to go in a van? Draw a picture
and write a sentence to answer the question.

SCHOOL-HOME CONNECTION With your child,
think of words, including names, that begin with *v*.

Special Times
Lesson 16   33

Harcourt

Name _____

▶ **Read each sentence. Circle the special name of a place. Then write it correctly.**

1. We like to walk up apple hill.

_____

- - - - - - - - - - - - - - - - - - - -

_____

2. Who got wet in pink pond?

_____

- - - - - - - - - - - - - - - - - - - -

_____

3. It's fun to play in rock park.

_____

- - - - - - - - - - - - - - - - - - - -

_____

4. We can eat at snack shop.

_____

- - - - - - - - - - - - - - - - - - - -

_____

TRY THIS Write the special name of a place you like to visit. Draw a picture of that place, too.

SCHOOL-HOME CONNECTION Let your child read aloud one of the special place names. Then help your child think of the special names of other places.

Harcourt

Name _____

▶ **Write a word from the box to complete each sentence.**

| each | play | says | Our |

1. We can _____ in the park.

2. _____ park is so much fun.

3. Kim _____, "I can catch you!"

4. We can _____ have a swing.

Harcourt

Name _____

▶ **Write a word from the box to complete each sentence.**

These	over	more	there

5. I can go up one _____ time.

6. I can go up and _____ the top.

7. Now we can play _____

over _____ .

8. _____ are good for digging.

 TRY THIS Write a sentence and then draw a picture about one thing you like to do with your friends. Use the word <u>play</u> in your writing.

Special Times
Lesson 17

SCHOOL-HOME CONNECTION Ask your child to read aloud the words in the boxes. Say a sentence, leaving out one of the vocabulary words. Have your child fill in the missing word.

Harcourt

Name _____

▶ **Look at each picture. Circle the word**
that completes the sentence. Then write the word.

yet   vet   vest

_____

— — — — — — — — —

1. Do we have to take Puff to the _____?

Yell   Tell   Yes

_____

— — — — — — — — —

2. _____, Puff is sick.

---

yam   yet   van

_____

— — — — — — — — —

3. Dad can take us in the _____.

TRY THIS Write your own sentence about Puff and the vet.
Draw a picture to go with your sentence.

SCHOOL-HOME CONNECTION Ask your child to identify and read aloud three words that begin with *v*. Then encourage your child to say other words that begin with the same sound.

Harcourt

Name _____

▶ **Circle the things that you learned in the story. Write them inside the circle of friends.**

You can talk with a friend.

Friends have to talk all the time.

Sometimes friends play.

Friends do not get mad at all.

It is fun to be a friend.

SCHOOL-HOME CONNECTION Ask your child to describe activities he or she likes to do with friends.

Harcourt

Name _____

▶ **Write the word that best completes each sentence.**

jumped   jumping

_____

- -

1. One frog _____ into the pond.

_____

jumps   jumping

_____

- -

2. Two more frogs are _____ in.

_____

look   looking

_____

- -

3. The big dog is _____.

_____

jumps   jumping

_____

- -

4. The big dog _____ in.

Harcourt

SCHOOL-HOME CONNECTION With your child, make up sentences
using the words *jump, jumps, jumped,* and *jumping.* See who can make
the silliest sentence.

▶ **Write the word from the box that best completes each sentence.**

her	fur	girl	purr	bird

_____
- - - - - - - - - - - - - -

1. The _____ stands still.

_____
- - - - - - - - - - - - - -

2. She sees a little _____.

_____
- - - - - - - - - - - - - -

3. Here comes _____ cat.

_____
- - - - - - - - - - - - - -

4. She pats the cat's _____.

_____
- - - - - - - - - - - - - -

5. The cat starts to _____.

SCHOOL-HOME CONNECTION Ask your child to read aloud the words in the box. Together, think of other words that contain the /ûr/ sound.

Harcourt

Name _____

▶ **Read each sentence. Circle the name of the day. Then write the name correctly.**

1. On monday we fed the pigs.

_____

_ _

_____

2. We fed the ducks on wednesday.

_____

_ _

_____

3. We went fishing on thursday.

_____

_ _

_____

_____

_ _

4. On friday we played! _____

Harcourt

◉**TRY**

THIS Write a sentence about your favorite day of the week. Use the name of the day in your sentence.

SCHOOL-HOME CONNECTION With your child, use a calendar to review the names of the days of the week.

Special Times
Lesson 21   **45**

Name _____

▶ **Write the word from the box that best completes each sentence.**

| around   use   myself |

_____

– – – – – – – – – – – – – – – –

1. "I can _____ some help here!"
   I cried.

_____

– – – – – – – – – – – – – – – –

2. My friends came and looked _____.

_____

– – – – – – – – – – – – – – – –

3. I had to get the mop all by _____.

 TRY THIS Write three other sentences about doing chores.
Use the words <u>use</u>, <u>around</u>, and <u>myself</u>.

Harcourt

Name _____

▶ **Write the word from the box that best completes each sentence.**

around   use   myself

_____

- - - - - - - - - - - - - - - - - -

4. "I can't do this by _____,"
I said.

5. "Can you find another mop to

_____

- - - - - - - - - - - - - - - - -

_____ ?" I asked.

_____

- - - - - - - - - - - - - - - - - -

6. Mitch looked all _____ for a mop.

Harcourt

▶ **Write the word from the box that best completes each sentence.**

first	purple	birds	ever	turns

_____

1. Five _____ are standing here.

_____

2. They will take _____.

_____

3. The _____ one is by the birdbath.

_____

4. Will she _____ go?

_____

5. A bird is _____.

 TRY THIS Write your own sentence about being first. Draw a picture to go with your sentence.

48 Special Times
Lesson 22

SCHOOL-HOME CONNECTION Encourage your child to suggest words that rhyme with *her*.

Harcourt

Name _____

▶ **Look at the pictures that show how to make a turnip pie. Tell the story by writing the sentences for the pictures.**

First, Digger Pig

_____

- -

_____

Then, Digger Pig

_____

- -

_____

Next, Digger Pig

_____

- -

_____

Last, Digger Pig

_____

- -

_____

Harcourt

TRY THIS Would you share the turnip pie with your friends?
Write a few sentences to tell why or why not.

SCHOOL-HOME CONNECTION Let your child help you prepare a
simple food. Talk about the steps as you follow the directions.

Special Times
Lesson 22   49

Name _____

▶ **Look at each picture. Circle the word that completes the sentence. Then write the word.**

hunch   lunch   match

_____

- - - - - - - - - - - - - - - - - - - -

1. What did you bring for _____?

such   crunch   bunch

_____

- - - - - - - - - - - - - - - - - - - -

2. I have a _____ of these.

much   such   switch

_____

- - - - - - - - - - - - - - - - - - - -

3. Do you want to _____?

Stitch   Catch   Batch

_____

- - - - - - - - - - - - - - - - - - - -

4. _____ these now!

TRY THIS Write a sentence with the word <u>much</u>. Draw a picture to go with your sentence.

SCHOOL-HOME CONNECTION With your child, list several things that are found in the *kitchen*.

Harcourt

Name _____

▶ **Look at the pictures and read the questions. Then write a sentence to answer each question.**

I. What does Stan do first?

_____

- - - - - - - - - - - - - - - - - - -

_____

2. What does he do next?

_____

- - - - - - - - - - - - - - - - - - -

_____

3. What does Stan do last?

_____

- - - - - - - - - - - - - - - - - - -

_____

Harcourt

Special Times
Lesson 23

▶ **Look at the picture. Choose a word
from the box that best completes each sentence.**

girl	dirt	fern	Her	curb

_____
- - - - - - - - - - - - - - - - - - - -

1. The _____ is planting.

_____
- - - - - - - - - - - - - - - - - - -

2. She is planting a _____.

_____
- - - - - - - - - - - - - - - - - - -

3. There she is on the _____.

_____   _____
- - - - - - - - - -   - - - - - - - - -

4. _____ hands are in the _____.

SCHOOL-HOME CONNECTION Write the word *hurt*,
and let your child read it aloud. Together, think of
other words that have the *ur* sound.

Harcourt

▶ **Finish each sentence. Add <u>er</u> or <u>est</u> to the word above the line.**

small
_____

- - - - - - - - - - - - - - - - - -

1. The fox is _____ than I am.

_____

near
_____

- - - - - - - - - - - - - - - - - -

2. You are _____ than I am.

_____

fast
_____

- - - - - - - - - - - - - - - - - -

3. The ostrich is the _____ bird.

_____

smart
_____

- - - - - - - - - - - - - - - - - -

4. I am the _____ of all.

SCHOOL-HOME CONNECTION Choose an object in your home.
Ask your child to find something that is *bigger* than the object.
Continue the game by having your child find other objects that are
bigger in your home.

Harcourt

► **Circle the word that completes each sentence. Then write the word.**

1. Our _____ reads about animals.

class
clip
cluck

2. We saw a _____ of birds.

clock
flick
flock

3. I think the birds need _____.

melt
help
gold

4. We _____ to find out about fish.

clap
plan
play

 TRY THIS Who, or what, do you like to play with? Write one or two sentences. If you want, draw a picture, too.

SCHOOL-HOME CONNECTION Ask your child to write or spell the word *flat*. Then ask your child to think of other words that begin with *fl*.

Harcourt

Name _____

▶ **Write the word from the box that best completes each sentence.**

goat	grow	slow	mow

1. Why does the grass

_____

- - - - - - - - - - - - - -

_____ so fast?

_____

- - - - - - - - - - - - - -

2. I wish it would _____ down.

_____

- - - - - - - - - - - - - -

3. I don't like to _____ the grass.

_____

- - - - - - - - - - - - - -

4. Would a _____

eat the grass?

TRY THIS Write a sentence with the word <u>boat</u>. Draw a picture to go with your sentence.

SCHOOL-HOME CONNECTION Encourage your child to suggest words that have the same sound you hear in the middle of the word *boat*.

Special Times
Lesson 25   **55**

Harcourt

Name _____

▶ **Read each sentence. Circle the name of the month. Then write the name correctly.**

1. Is it cold in january?

_____

- - - - - - - - - - - - - - - - - - -

_____

2. Do foxes put on vests in february?

_____

- - - - - - - - - - - - - - - - - - -

_____

3. Do they take off their hats in april?

_____

- - - - - - - - - - - - - - - - - - -

_____

4. Is august too hot?

_____

- - - - - - - - - - - - - - - - - - -

_____

TRY THIS Write a sentence about the month you like best. Draw a picture to go with your sentence.

Special Times
56 Lesson 26

SCHOOL-HOME CONNECTION With your child, use a calendar to review the names of the months. Then help your child write the name of his or her birthday month.

Harcourt

Name _____

▶ **Read the words in the box. Write the word that best completes each sentence.**

teacher	how	ready

1. Miss Pat said, "I am your new

_____

_____

_____. "

_____

_____

2. "Are you _____ to help me?"

_____

_____

3. "Let's find out _____ to do a jig!"

 TRY THIS Draw a picture of something you could show a friend how to do. Write a sentence about your picture.

▶ **Read the words in the box. Write the word that best completes each sentence.**

music	dance	shall

_____

- -

4. "What _____ we do first?"

_____

- -

5. "We can play the _____."

6. Now, we can do the steps to

_____

- - - - - - - - - - - - - - - - - - -

the _____.

SCHOOL-HOME CONNECTION With your child, talk about something he or she likes to do, and some new things he or she may want to learn to do.

Harcourt

▶ **Choose the correct column for each word in the box. Write the word under boat or crow.**

| snow | coat | road | soap | bowl | yellow |

boat

crow

_____ _____

- - - - - - - - - - - - - - - - - - - - - - - - - - - - - - - -

_____ _____

- - - - - - - - - - - - - - - - - - - - - - - - - - - - - - - -

_____ _____

- - - - - - - - - - - - - - - - - - - - - - - - - - - - - - - -

_____ _____

SCHOOL-HOME CONNECTION With your child, write a
short poem with words that contain long vowel /ō/
spelled *oa* and *ow*.

Harcourt

Name _____

▶ **Think about the story and fill in the chart.**

What Did Rex Think?

What Time Is It?   **What Did Rex Do?**

What Time Is It?	What Did Rex Think? / What Did Rex Do?
Time for dance class	
Time to warm up	
Time to dance	
Time to go home	

60 Special Times
Lesson 27

SCHOOL-HOME CONNECTION Ask your child to tell you about the story "Rex and Lilly Playtime."

Harcourt

Name _____

Phonics

R-controlled Vowels:
/är/ar, /ôr/or
Long Vowel:
/ō/ow, oa

▶ **Read the letter. Write the word that best completes each sentence.**

Dear Meg,

more   morning

_____

I had fun this _____.

car   corn

_____

My dad and I washed the _____.

snow   soap

_____

The _____ got on my dog.

snow   show

_____

It looked like _____! You can

help next time!

Your friend,
Margaret

MAIL

SCHOOL-HOME CONNECTION Have your child point out the word *snow* on this page. With your child, take turns making up other sentences using the word *snow*.

Special Times
Lesson 28   **61**

Harcourt

▶ **Read the three paragraphs. Number them in story order. Write a title for the story.**

_____

- -

_____

 At last they came to the top. "Oh, good," cried Stork. "We are here!" They jumped onto the sled. Down they went. "What a ride!" they said.

 Rabbit and Stork walked and walked up the hill. It was a very big hill. They felt tired.

Rabbit wanted to go sledding. He called Stork and said, "Come to the hill. Bring your sled."

SCHOOL-HOME CONNECTION Let your child tell you what happened first, next, and last in the story about Rabbit and Stork. Then have them draw a picture that tells what might happen next.

Harcourt

Name _____

▶ **Finish each sentence. Put together the word and the word ending above the line. Write that new word on the line.**

play + ing

_____

- - - - - - - - - - - - - - - - - - - -

1. The girls are _____ on the beach.

---

pick + ing

_____

- - - - - - - - - - - - - - - - - - - -

2. Dan is _____ up shells.

---

help + ed

_____

- - - - - - - - - - - - - - - - - - - -

3. At first, Carmen _____ Dan.

---

run + s

_____

- - - - - - - - - - - - - - - - - - - -

4. Her dog _____ in the sand.

Harcourt

▶ **Circle the sentence that tells about the picture.**

1. The pig sat on a cat.

The pig put on a coat.

The pigs pat the cot.

2. The pig got the bat.

The pig put on a hat.

The pig got into the boat.

3. The pig said hello to the coat.

The pig said hello to the cat.

The pig said hello to the cot.

4. A goat ran up to the cat.

A goat ran with a cut.

A coat was on the cat.

5. The goat got into the boat.

The goat got onto the cot.

The cat got into the boat.

Harcourt

SCHOOL-HOME CONNECTION Choose one of the pictures, and ask your child to read all three sentence choices. Encourage your child to tell how he or she identified the correct sentence.

Little Chicks Hatch

Is there much time left?

When will your eggs hatch?

Harcourt

The other hens are happy.

8 The chicks will be hens soon.

Look, your first little

chick wiggles out.

6

"Cackle! Cackle!" flaps the hen.

2 Her eggs are going to hatch.

— Fold —

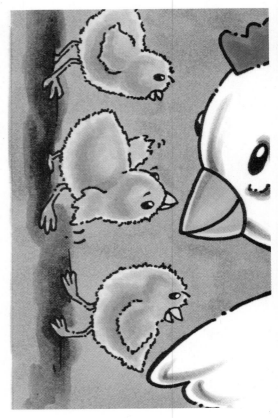

Three little chicks are on their feet. They hop and peck.

7

4 the little chicks will come out.

Now the hen hides her eggs. Soon

— Fold —

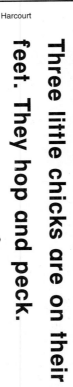

Chip! Chip! Crack! Crack!
One by one the eggs hatch.

5

Kristen Sells Stars

1

Fold

Harcourt

Kristen will sell some yarn stars. 3

Fold

Kristen sells every star. Nothing
is left. She is very happy!

8

"Yes," says Kristen.
"I made them this week."

6

4

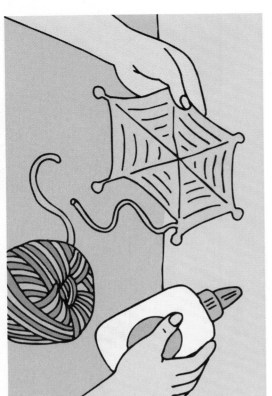

One star is not right.
Kristen can fix it.

2

It is market day at the barn.
The cars park in the yard.

"We like your stars.
Did you make them?"

5

"I will take two stars—one for
my sister and one for me."

7

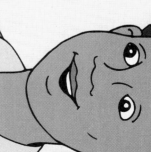

Fold

Fold

Who Am I?

1

I don't have any time to stop.
I always just buzz about.

3

Fold — Harcourt — Fold

What little bug am I?

8

**Why must you watch out for me?
I can sting you!**

6

4

I am quick to fly away
when you come by.

2

I am a buzzing bug. I buzz
from blossom to blossom.

— Fold —

— Fold —

Harcourt

I have six legs that
can jump and walk.

5

If I hum by you,
just run away.

7

A Jumping Green Pet

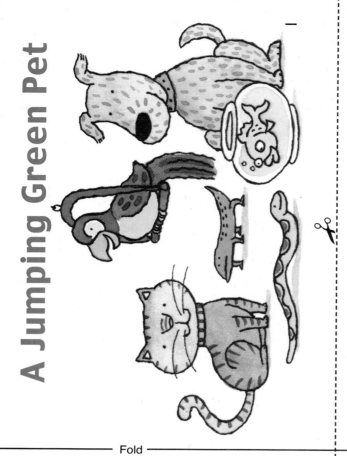

1

Harcourt

Fold

Do you want
a little bug?
Each of these
can jump far.

3

Fold

Yes! I like
this pet a
lot. It's
green and it
can jump!

8

If I had seven more
of these, not one
could jump.

6

Well, some bugs are green, but they're not what I want to play with.

I want a green pet that can jump.

Harcourt

— Fold —

— Fold —

I've a green animal here. Why don't you look at it?

Here is a pet you're going to like. It came from over there.

Twirling Around!

Who can twirl the fastest?
Who can jump the longest?

Harcourt

--- Fold ---

--- Fold ---

Let's stop twirling around
and brush off this dirt.

Look at the dust!
Look at all of this dirt!

4

Turn to the right! Faster! Faster!

Let's twirl around!
Let's jump up and down!

2

Harcourt

Fold

Fold

Turn to the left!
Use your two feet.

My shirt has dirt on it!
My skirt has dirt on it!

5

7

A Load of Stuff

Fold

Harcourt

"What did you put in here?" groaned Goat. "I packed good things for us to munch on," said Toad.

Fold

Show what Toad packed in the basket.

Goat picked up the basket, and the two friends went on.

"Are you ready, Toad?"
asked Goat. "I want to swim!"

Goat lifted the basket and
they walked down the road.

--- Fold ---

--- Fold ---

"How about some lunch now?"
asked Toad. "The stuff looks
good!"

"This basket is full," he said. "I'll
rest over here." Then Toad asked,
"Shall we go now?"

Skills and Strategies Index

COMPREHENSION

Classifying **L1** 49, 70
Drawing Conclusions **L2** 10, 20
Noting Details **L2** 50, 62
Reality/Fantasy **L3** 10, 30

Retell and Summarize **L1** 15, 25, 35, 46,
    57, 67 **L2** 7, 17, 28, 37, 47, 59, 60
    L3 7, 17, 27, 38, 49, 60
Sequence **L1** 18, 28 **L3** 40, 62

GRAMMAR

Asking Sentences **L1** 53
Complete Sentences **L2** 33
Names of Days **L3** 45
Names of Months **L3** 56
Naming Parts for
    Two People or Things **L2** 3
Naming Parts of Sentences **L1** 63
Nouns **L2** 45
Nouns: Animals or Things **L3** 3
Nouns: People or Places **L2** 55

One and More Than One **L3** 13
Sentences **L1** 9, 21
Special Names and Titles
    for People **L3** 23
Special Names of Places **L3** 34
Telling Parts for Two Things That
    Someone or Something Does **L2** 24
Telling Parts of Sentences **L2** 13
Telling Sentences **L1** 41
Word Order **L1** 31

PHONICS

Consonants
    /b/*b* **L2** 32, 36, 39
    /k/*c* **L1** 26, 27, 69
    /d/*d* **L1** 40, 45, 56
    /d/*dd* **L2** 18, 19
    /f/*f, ff* **L2** 29, 30, 61
    /g/*g* **L2** 12, 16, 46
    /h/*h* **L1** 36, 37, 45
    /j/*j* **L3** 28, 29, 41
    /k/*k, ck* **L1** 58, 59
    /l/*l, ll* **L1** 62, 66
    /l/*-le* **L3** 8, 9
    /m/*m* **L1** 9, 17, 24
    /n/*n* **L1** 52, 56, 59
    /n/*nn* **L2** 18, 19
    /p/*p* **L1** 30, 34, 48
    /r/*r* **L2** 23, 27, 36
    /s/*s* **L1** 16, 17, 37
    /s/*ss* **L2** 18, 19
    /t/*t* **L1** 20, 24, 34
    /t/*tt* **L2** 18, 19
    /v/*v* **L3** 33, 37, 39
    /w/*w* **L2** 42, 46, 58
    /x/*x* **L2** 60, 61
    /y/*y* **L3** 18, 19, 37
    /z/*z, zz* **L3** 28, 29, 41

Digraphs
    /ch/*ch, tch* **L3** 6, 50
    /kw/*qu* **L3** 28, 29, 41
    /sh/*sh* **L2** 48, 49, 58
    /th/*th* **L2** 8, 9, 46

Blends
    l **L3** 11, 31, 54
    r **L2** 31, 41, 64
    s **L2** 11, 40, 63

Contractions
    '*ll* **L2** 52
    n't **L1** 71
    '*ve, 're* **L3** 42

Inflections
    -er, -est **L3** 53
    -es, -ed, -ing **L2** 21, 51
    -'s, -ed, -ing **L1** 38, 72 **L3** 20, 43, 63

Phonograms
    -ang, -ong **L2** 22
    -ap, -at **L1** 39
    -arn, -orn **L3** 21
    -at, -nam **L1** 29
    -ick, -ack **L1** 61

Skills and Strategies Index

VOCABULARY